2,4,6,8

This Is How We Regulate!

75 Play Therapy Activities to Increase
Mindfulness in Children

Tracy Turner-Bumberry, LPC,RPT-S,CAS

2,4,6,8 This is How We Regulate! © copyright 2019 by Tracy Turner-Bumberry.

Published by:
PESI Publishing & Media
PESI, Inc.
3839 White Ave.
Eau Claire, WI 54703

Cover Design: Amy Rubenzer
Editing By: Michelle Nelson
Layout: Amy Rubenzer

Printed in the United States of America
ISBN: 9781683731733

PESI
Publishing
& Media
publishing.pesi.com

About the Author

Tracy Turner-Bumberry, MA, LPC, RPT-S, CAS, is the owner/operator of KS Counseling, LLC. Tracy is a Licensed Professional Counselor, a Registered Play Therapist-Supervisor, a Certified AutPlay Therapist/Trainer, and a Certified Autism Specialist. She has over twenty years of experience working with children, adolescents, and young adults.

Tracy has been in private practice since 2009. Prior to working in private practice, Tracy worked as a high school teacher and an elementary school counselor. She is an expert at interpreting and explaining school procedures and documents to parents, especially in the area of Individual Educational Programs (IEP's). In addition to her private practice, Tracy is a certified AutPlay Trainer, and conducts Play Therapy workshops across the country.

Table of Contents

Foreword

I recall presenting to a group of professional adults who worked for a large trucking company. The human resources department had invited me to come to their national headquarters and present two trainings on mindfulness. The headquarters happened to be in Arkansas and a few days before the presentations, I received a call from the organization facilitating my presentations. Among other things, they wanted to remind me that I was going into a trucking company and many of these adults may not know what mindfulness is or may not take it seriously. They recommended that I change the language to something like stress reduction, which might be better received. I considered the recommendation but decided I was going to be true to mindfulness and do my best to make it relevant to these folks working at this trucking company.

In my many years of conducting presentations of all kinds and sizes, I can safely say that I have never experienced a group of adults more attentive and focused on what I was speaking about and more engaged in the interventions we were doing together. Several attendees talked with me after the presentations, expressing their satisfaction with the content. Many expressed they had been asking their company to do something like this and bring more mindfulness into the work environment. Not only did so many of these attendees want this information, they needed it. For me, this experience solidified the yearning for so many of us to find presence, peace, and the ability to be fully in our moments, to throw off judgment, and to feel relaxed.

The ability to help present and implement mindfulness into a person's life is truly a special gift—and much more rewarding, to be a part of helping children gain this ability—a life changing and lifelong way of healthy living. I was so excited to see this book from Tracy Turner-Bumberry—a clearly communicated, playful guide to help children learn and practice mindfulness. I was honored and more than willing to provide a foreword for this important resource. Tracy has presented mindfulness in an easy-to-understand format that can apply smoothly for children. She provides the necessary overview of mindfulness and play therapy, including how to create mindfulness play therapy interventions. Each intervention is clearly presented with a brief description, materials needed, and bulleted step-by-step instructions.

Play therapists and any professional who works with children will find these interventions engaging and effective. I have used several with the clients that I work with and so many children love the interventions and request to do them again and again. Interventions such as *Jump into the Picture*—are you ready? 1-2-3, let's jump into the picture—are fun, playful, and right on point in helping children understand and implement mindfulness into their life. If we all could have been fortunate enough to play these activities and learn these mindfulness approaches as children, how rewarding and healthy that would have been. Tracy has created a valuable resource to do just that for this and future generations.

—Dr. Robert Jason Grant
Author and creator of AutPlay® therapy for children and
adolescents on the autism spectrum

Introduction

What is more joyful than a child engaging in play? Play is a child's natural language and so often expresses what words simply cannot. Play allows a child to be in the present, fully immersed in the task at hand. Mindfulness is a sharp focus on the present moment, being attentive yet non-judgmental. Practicing mindfulness daily can help individuals of any age achieve happiness, inner peace, and improved emotion regulation. What better way for a child to experience mindfulness than through play? Yet, so often we try to teach mindfulness to children through words and directives, heavy on the verbal, with little imagination or creativity involved. This can be challenging for a neurotypical child but almost impossible for children who we often see in our therapy rooms. The children we see with emotion regulation issues—children with autism spectrum disorder, anxiety, and ADHD—have an extremely difficult time learning mindful techniques verbally. **Play therapy is integral towards creating mindful children who improve their emotion regulation skills.** Using this expressive arts therapy will allow a child to have fun, play, and reach a greater state of regulation. The focus of this book is to provide the reader with a variety of play therapy interventions to promote mindfulness in children. You may be wondering how this workbook is different than any of the other multitudes of books you can find on mindfulness. Here are some things that make this workbook unique.

PLAY THERAPY FOCUS

Many current mindfulness interventions are verbal in description and contain a lot of dialogue. If we were to simply explain mindfulness to children, they would most likely tune out well before we were finished! For most clients, speaking to a grown-up is not their idea of fun! Children want to experience things in a fun and entertaining way by using their senses and their bodies. They often do a lot of sitting and focusing in school and at home doing homework, so they certainly do not want to sit and listen in the therapy room, too! Children respond best through play therapy techniques—be it art, movement, or nature based. Children will be more excited to try these interventions with a play therapy focus—and continue to want to practice them—because they are fun and meaningful to them. Whenever any mindful technique is continually practiced, we can begin to see more mindful children!

INTERVENTIONS ARE SIMPLE AND EASY TO REPLICATE

Many of you reading this book may not be play therapists with a dedicated play therapy office. Some of you may not even have an office! In my travels presenting to various professionals in the helping fields, I have learned that we are quite the resourceful bunch! Some of you are in tiny rooms, several different rooms, or in clients' homes. Some of you travel to various locations throughout the day and do not have the ability to carry a large amount of materials to complete detailed interventions with clients. Others of you may see your clients so briefly (maybe two or three sessions) that you need resources that are easy for the client to replicate at home and at school.

Every intervention presented in this workbook will be simple, require few materials, and be easy for you to explain to the child, parent, school teacher, or to other therapists. You will not need to be a Registered Play Therapist to complete these interventions. Of course, I highly recommend seeking training in play therapy, and working towards your Registered Play Therapist credential will allow you to stand out in your field. I do understand, however, that this is not possible for everyone, so I feel it is important to provide all child professionals with play-based interventions to use in sessions.

MEANINGFUL INTERVENTIONS

I have used play therapy mindful interventions as a school counselor, as a Registered Play Therapist-Supervisor in an inpatient psychiatric hospital, and in my current private practice. Therefore, I have directly seen these interventions work when practiced with children. They have found them to be such fun and have actually wanted to practice them at home and at school! Children often want me to teach their entire family so everyone can be involved!

I have also taught these interventions to thousands of participants who come to my training seminars, and I have experienced the joy of reading emails from workshop participants stating, "It really did work!" I have witnessed new motivation and excitement from child professionals who have been feeling stuck in their fields. This is as rewarding as when I notice healing in my clients!

Because these interventions have been used regularly by many and have shown positive results, I believe that the interventions I have included are very beneficial towards clients' overall health and growth. These are not simply a hodge-podge of activities, but a meaningful collection of mindfulness-based play therapy interventions. They were chosen carefully by me as interventions that are not only the most fun for clients, but also the ones that have seemed to produce the deepest levels of mindfulness. Having this collection of mindful interventions should greatly enhance your work with your clients!

IT'S NOT ALL ABOUT BREATHING

Many resources about mindfulness teach a variety of breathing techniques; some of these resources focus entirely on mindful breathing. While this is important for children to learn, most of our clients easily bore from breathing interventions and therefore do not want to practice them. I've had my fair share of clients resist learning about any type of mindful breathing, stating they've learned it before and it "doesn't work." I will explain five breathing techniques to help create a calmer physical body, but just five. The five chosen are by far the most popular ones I have used with my clients and are also the ones reported as the most successful by the participants in the trainings I have conducted. These breathing techniques can be practiced before the child completes any of the play therapy mindful interventions to further enhance the experience.

If you are a child therapist, psychologist, occupational therapist, or special education teacher looking for ways to increase mindfulness in the children you work with, while having fun, then this workbook is for you. These interventions are simple, require few materials, and will be joyful to complete and replicate. My sincere hope is for readers to find this workbook easy to understand, practical to use, and beneficial towards their clients' growth. I thank you for choosing this book and wish you great health and happiness on your journey towards mindfulness within yourself and your clients!

1
Play Therapy

"Enter into children's play and you will find the place where their minds, hearts, and souls meet."
—Virginia Axline,
Pioneer of Play Therapy

Imagine young Johnny visiting a therapist's office for the first time. He isn't sure why he has to be there, although he does know that many people in his life are making him mad. His mom has said that this counselor will help him with his anger, so he thinks it can't be all that bad. Johnny arrives at the counselor's office, which consists of a room, a couch, two chairs, and various (boring to Johnny) décor. The counselor introduces herself and then begins asking Johnny about his anger, his anger triggers, his coping mechanisms, etc. How responsive do you think Johnny would be to these questions? Do you believe Johnny would feel comfortable sharing his experiences with this counselor—an adult he has just met? Do you think Johnny even has the words to fully express what he is feeling? As an adult, how often have you had difficulty finding the right words to fully explain your challenging experiences? I imagine Johnny is hearing the counselor's words much as the classic Peanuts characters hear the adults in their lives, "Wah, wah, wah, wah…" (Please watch any of the Charlie Brown movies if you are unaware of this reference!). Johnny may have various answers, such as "I don't know," "I'm not sure," or maybe no words at all but simply a shrug of his shoulders. This counselor may then view Johnny's reactions as resistant, closed, or non-committal, when actually Johnny just doesn't really know or understand exactly what the counselor is asking! We can suspect that Johnny will most likely not want to visit this counselor again.

Now imagine Johnny visiting a play therapist's office for the first time. He, again, isn't sure why he has to go there, but people are still making him as mad as ever! His mom repeats that this counselor will help him with his anger, so he decides to give it another go. He arrives at the counselor's office, but this time he enters a colorful room filled with toys! There is a sandbox, a dollhouse, puppets, an art station, and various games. The walls are filled with child-centered art work, and there is no sign of a couch or adult seating.

The counselor introduces herself and invites Johnny to explore the room and play with whatever he wants. She engages with him, laughs with him, and actually plays with him! He goes right to the swords, and boy does it feel good to slam these swords into a punching bag! He can feel intense feelings rising, then dissolving the more he hits the bag with the sword. This session is fun! Johnny can't believe his time is almost up when the counselor gives him the five-minute warning; then, when the session is over, he runs out of the office to tell his mom about the fun he had.

What do you believe has been Johnny's experience this time? Do you believe he is comfortable with this therapist? Do you believe he will want to return? More importantly, do you believe that at this very first session Johnny experienced some healing without having to articulate his issue? If you answered a resounding "Yes!" then you are indeed ready to use play therapy interventions in your practice.

WHAT IS PLAY THERAPY?

The Association for Play Therapy (APT) defines play therapy as "the systematic use of a theoretical model to establish an interpersonal process wherein trained play therapists use the therapeutic powers of play to help clients prevent or resolve psychosocial difficulties and achieve optimal growth and development" (a4pt.org, 2016). In play therapy, clients express themselves through carefully selected toys provided by the play therapist. **Play is considered to be the child's natural language to promote insight and healing.** Children play what they know, and their play can help therapists more fully understand the world of the child.

An example I like to use to highlight the personal nature of play involves a dollhouse and miniatures. Let's say I presented you with a dollhouse, and outside of this dollhouse several dollhouse miniatures. These miniature people are a variety of colors, sizes, genders, and shapes representative of society. If I were to ask you to choose whichever miniatures you would like to place in the dollhouse, which would you choose? Think about this before continuing. Most likely your choices would be based on your family of origin or your current nuclear family. If I were to then invite you to play with these miniatures, how would this play look? Again, spend some time thinking about this. Quite possibly, your play would entail a recent happening, a past memory, or a troubling situation. Your play would likely be representative of something real to you. (Yes, even adults play what we know!) My dollhouse play may be quite different than yours, representing my own personal experiences.

I'll never forget a 3-year-old client of mine whose dollhouse play involved the police coming to take the boy miniature away from his mother. It was a full 15 minutes of unscripted, deliberate, heartbreaking play. Talking later to his caseworker, I discovered this was exactly what had happened to him several months ago. Would I have discovered this by asking him about himself, his family, his family life? I believe the answer is a definite "No." But, through play therapy, he could express his hurt and confusion over losing his mom in a safe, caring environment. Children around the world can express their needs, their desires, their hurts, their goals, and so much more without the confusion of language when they engage in play therapy.

VARIOUS APPROACHES TO PLAY THERAPY

Within the play therapy model, there are several different approaches to how play is used in the therapy room. Simply stated, play therapy approaches are on a spectrum—from complete non-directive/non-structured methods to highly directive and structured methods. Just talking to one registered play therapist or attending one play therapy training will most certainly not scratch the surface of the many play therapy models! A brief discussion on the variances between non-directive and directive—while also mentioning that many play therapists are eclectic/prescriptive in nature and move between the models depending on their clients—is necessary for the reader to dig a little deeper into the world of play therapy.

Non-directive/non-structured play therapy believes that the child ultimately possesses the capability to determine the course of the sessions. The therapist's role is to create a safe environment, show the client unconditional positive regard, and reflect possible emotions the client is feeling. The therapist does set boundaries and limits in the playroom in areas such as time, safety, and destruction of toys. Insight is gained by the child working out any maladaptive emotions and behaviors with a wide variety of toys—carefully selected by the therapist and representing categories such as nurturing, aggressive, expressive, and fantasy. The most well-known non-directive style of play therapy is Child Centered Play Therapy developed by Dr. Garry Landreth. His seminal book entitled *Play Therapy: The Art of the Relationship* (3rd ed., 2012) is an excellent resource for anyone interested in learning more about non-directive play therapy.

Directive/structured methods of play therapy involve a more directed approach and planning by the play therapist to guide the course of the client's sessions. Thoughtful interventions and objectives are planned based on the client's diagnosis, presenting problems, and needs. The directive play therapy room may range from being well-stocked with carefully selected toys to being an empty room with the only toys brought in being those that are needed for the intervention. Examples of a more directive approach include Theraplay, Cognitive Behavioral Play Therapy, and Adlerian Play Therapy. Therapists interested in this type of approach should be able to find several useful publications and trainings on the directive model for more information.

Somewhere along the spectrum of non-directive/non-structured approaches and directive/structured approaches are eclectic approaches to play therapy. **Electic approaches** focus on the client at hand and determine the best approach for them based upon the therapist's knowledge base, personality, and current research in the field. These play therapists are committed to gaining a wealth of knowledge in all play therapy models and attend a variety of trainings from different approaches. These therapists need to not vacillate between models in a random manner, but carefully choose the right approach based on each client's diagnosis, presenting problems, and needs.

One important note: because this book focuses on mindful play therapy interventions, the assumption could be made that the readers attempting these interventions will be using a directive approach. Although this is true—at least initially when the therapist is teaching the child these activities—it is important to note that, once learned, the therapist may want to take a less structured approach and allow the client to fully direct the flow of the session. By doing this, the client can choose what he or she truly needs in that moment to best self-regulate.

BENEFITS OF PLAY THERAPY

There are enormous benefits to using play therapy with children of all ages. According to the Association for Play Therapy (and personal experience) these include helping clients to:

- Become more responsible for behaviors and develop more successful strategies
- Develop new and creative solutions to problems
- Develop respect and acceptance of self and others
- Learn to experience and express emotion
- Cultivate empathy and respect for the thoughts and feelings of others
- Learn new social skills and relational skills with family
- Develop self-efficacy and thus a better assuredness about their abilities

PLAY THERAPY INTERVENTIONS IN THIS BOOK

As a Registered Play Therapist-Supervisor, I cannot express enough the great value in becoming a registered play therapist. Having the specific training and rigorous development in play therapy allows therapists to be competent, highly-valued members of a child's team. A dedicated play room is ideal as well, stocked with a variety of carefully selected items. However, any therapist can use playful interventions to help clients feel calmer, more peaceful, and self-regulated! I took special care in choosing interventions that are simple to understand, easy to practice, and able to be replicated in a variety of settings. I was particularly careful to choose interventions with a minimal amount of materials and materials that would be relatively inexpensive to purchase. Given that these interventions promote mindfulness in clients, I want to ensure that they can be done in a variety of settings—beyond the therapy room into their homes, schools, playgrounds, and more! You can rest assured that no matter your current level of knowledge on play therapy, you will be able to use these interventions successfully!

ONE FINAL THOUGHT

I want to emphasize that the interventions in this book can help ANYONE become more mindful and regulated. I invite YOU to practice these, no matter what your age or ability level. I often say in my trainings that we cannot expect our clients to be mindful if we ourselves are not mindful! Don't hesitate to complete each of these interventions yourself before even practicing them with your clients. You may be surprised how much calmer you feel as a result.

Mindfulness

"Life is a dance. Mindfulness is witnessing the dance."
—Amit Ray,
Author & Philosopher

When I think about mindfulness, I remember a cartoon I once saw of a man walking his dog. The caption under the man says, "Mind full" and shows a bubble above the man's head filled with images of bills, to-do lists, and other daily stressors. The caption under the dog say "Mindful" and the bubble above the dog's head shows exactly what he is looking at ahead of him. What a perfect idea of what mindfulness is! Understanding mindfulness is one small part of the equation; practicing mindfulness is quite a different endeavor. It is my strong belief, however, that we cannot expect to have regulated and mindful clients if we ourselves are not regulated and mindful. For this reason, it's beneficial to have a chapter describing what mindfulness is and how we can all begin to achieve mindfulness.

WHAT IS MINDFULNESS?

In recent years, mindfulness has become popular with the general public, and many have discovered the great benefits of a mindfulness practice. However, many are also confused about mindfulness and often mistake it for a religious or spiritual practice. Therefore, a brief explanation of mindfulness is needed in this book to help illuminate the role of mindful play therapy interventions towards clients' emotion regulation. Readers will notice that all of the interventions in this book have a mindfulness component to them, but therapists can follow a couple of guidelines to create mindful interventions on their own.

A general definition of mindfulness I use is from Jon Kabat-Zinn, a psychologist often known as the "father of mindfulness." (I highly recommend reading any of his books to more fully learn about this topic.) In his book *Wherever You Go, There You Are: Mindfulness Meditation in Everyday Life* (1997), **Kabat-Zinn defines mindfulness as "An attentive, non-judgmental focus on experiences in the here and now."**

Looking closely at this definition, we could view "attentive" as being aware and engaged with whatever is happening in our lives in the present moment. How often do we go through our lives as if we are on autopilot? We walk, drive, sit, stand, talk, and more without any awareness of what is currently happening! Being aware is being present, slowing down, and recognizing where we are.

The word "non-judgmental" is crucial to remember when practicing awareness. We want to be in the present moment without judging the present moment. It is part of our habit energy to judge an experience as "good" or "bad" with various levels within the two extremes. If we are having a good experience, we may try too hard to hold on to it and become anxious about the experience ending (which, obviously, it will have to come to an end!). This grasping prevents us from fully being mindful in the moment. On the other hand, if we label an experience as bad, we often try to run away from it, push past it, or ruminate about it endlessly. We forget that this experience is temporary and become afraid it won't end, thereby forgetting the present experience. When practicing viewing experiences with a non-judgmental mind, we "sit" with whatever we are experiencing, not viewing it as good nor bad, but just as it is.

If we can remember these two words, **attentive** and **non-judgmental**, we are well on our way of achieving a mindful state of mind.

A factor analysis of several mindfulness questionnaires showed the following five descriptors as commonly perceived aspects of mindfulness (Baer et al., 2006). These descriptors may also help the reader understand mindfulness.

1. Observing one's experiences
2. Describing them
3. Acting with awareness
4. Non-judging of inner experience
5. Non-reactivity to inner experience

These factors show the important work that is needed to keep one's mind open, honest, and free from judgement. Being able to first observe, next describe, and then act with awareness—all the while not judging the experience—is not something that comes natural to any of us. It is through consistent and routine practice that we will discover ourselves becoming mindful. We should not view this as a race, where being fully mindful is the finish line. Rather, we can work on becoming a little more mindful at a time, perhaps accepting that we may never be fully mindful at all! Finding times throughout the day to work on mindfulness can be a great starting point towards a more mindful state of being. Practitioners will notice that this becomes easier and begins occurring more naturally with time and continued practice.

BENEFITS OF MINDFULNESS

Practicing mindfulness has proven to provide many individual benefits, including reducing stress and anxiety (Kabat-Zinn et al., 1992), reducing depression (Ma & Teasdale, 2004), and enhancing personal awareness (Langer, 2012). Increases in mindfulness have also shown a significant correlation with the reduction of avoidance and rumination (Kumar et al., 2008), as well as an overall sense of greater health and less pain. Research has indicated that mindfulness methods may contribute to overall health because these activities alter organization and action of neural circuitry, which is associated with alterations in reactions to stress and immune function (Davidson et al., 2003). In addition, recent studies have shown that applying mindfulness in parenting improves the relationship between parent and child, as well as the stress level of the parents (Beer et al., 2013). Several studies have also shown that mindfulness-based practices with adolescents resulted in improvements with attention, internalizing and externalizing behavior problems, anxiety, and academic performance (Beauchemin, Hutchins, & Patterson, 2008).

Further research is needed to determine the full benefits of mindfulness interventions with children, as ideas such as sustained attention and meditation may be too difficult for children to accomplish. Younger children need reduced time, more props, and more movement when attempting mindfulness interventions. There have been positive results shown with children learning mindfulness through movement, such as yoga, or through art and play activities. A study of preschool-aged children participating in a year-long mindful yoga practice showed significant increases in self-regulation (Razza et al., 2015), and a study of 9- to 13-year-olds using Mindfulness Based Cognitive Therapy for Children (MBCT-C) found that the children participating had fewer attention problems and less anxiety after completing the interventions (Semple, 2010). The authors noted that these mindfulness practices utilized more movement, activities, and play due to the age of the participants. Play therapy interventions focusing on mindfulness seem to be both a fun and beneficial way for children to be able to "feel" mindfulness and replicate it into a viable practice.

CREATING A MINDFULNESS-BASED PLAY THERAPY INTERVENTION

Greenberg and Harris (2011) mention three ways that therapeutic interventions have a focus on mindfulness: by sharpening concentration or attention, building emotion regulation skills to properly handle stress, and developing a positive self-concept. I believe many play therapy interventions can do these very things. If you want to test out any intervention to determine its level of mindfulness, these questions may be very useful:

Sharpening Concentration:

- Does this intervention allow for complete focus?
- Is the intervention developmentally appropriate for the client?
- Is the intervention multi-sensory?
- Does the intervention allow for fine or gross motor movement?
- Is the intervention fun for the client?

Building Emotion Regulation Skills:

- Will the intervention allow for various emotions to be experienced?
- Is there a degree of appropriate challenge, which could promote success?
- Can the client modify the intervention if needed?
- Can positive coping skills be discovered when completing this intervention?
- Can the meaning of the intervention be applicable to other settings?

Developing a Positive Self-Concept:

- Will the intervention highlight client strengths?
- Will the client feel successful from completing the intervention?
- Will the intervention allow for connection between therapist and client?
- Will the client be able to use his/her imagination and creativity to lead the intervention?
- Does the intervention help the client feel good?

A BRIEF NOTE ABOUT INTERVENTIONS

It is important to note that all of the interventions detailed in this book help the client have fun, be engaged, and feel good, but interventions are most certainly not one-size-fits-all! The cornerstone of client growth and success is the relationship between the therapist and the client. Clients must feel accepted, safe, and valued by their therapists before any intervention can be effective. Interventions are absolutely no substitute for the connection between therapist and client. Once this relationship is established, however, mindful interventions can be one of the many tools in a therapist's toolbox to help promote client success.

Using Mindful Play Therapy Interventions With Autism, Anxiety, and ADHD Clients

"We are survivors the moment of diagnosis."
—Peter Jennings

Children with autism, anxiety, and ADHD often have more emotion regulation difficulties than neurotypical children. Using mindful play therapy interventions with children who have these diagnoses can be a practical way for them to improve attention, a positive self-concept, and increased emotional control. Here is a brief review to more fully understand the importance of using mindful play therapy interventions with these groups of children.

AUTISM

The expression, "Show me a child with autism, and I'll know about one child with autism" rings true when discussing Autism Spectrum Disorder (ASD). ASD is indeed on a spectrum, and the strengths and challenges with one child on the spectrum may be quite different from another. However, there are some key factors noticed with those individuals on the autism spectrum that we can safely predict to see in the therapy room. According to the CDC (2017), some common symptoms of ASD include:

Social Skills Difficulty: This is different than a child who may be shy or withdrawn. Children on the autism spectrum tend to prefer playing alone, misunderstand group dynamics, and may miss important facial expressions and other non-verbal gestures in others. These children may not share the same interests as their peers and may not enjoy typical childhood games involving physical contact. They may also have great difficulty with personal space and cooperation.

Communication Difficulty: Although children with ASD vary in the degree of communication difficulties they may have, all possess some type of communication deficits. Up to 40% of children on the spectrum do not speak at all. Others may have speech and language difficulties, including a flat/monotone voice when speaking, pronoun reversals, and frequent repetition of words and phrases (echolalia). Children with ASD often do not answer questions appropriately, or may talk at length about a subject they are interested in, without pausing to allow others to speak, or checking to see if the other person is interested. Sarcasm, jokes, and humor may be very difficult for a child with ASD to understand.

Unusual Interests and Behaviors: Children with ASD are often seen as "odd" or "weird" to neurotypical children. ASD children tend to be highly interested in things that do not interest their peers (examples may include vacuum cleaners, ships, trains, etc.). They may be especially interested in the parts that make up these objects, and can become regimented in learning about them. They often will do the same play routines (such as taking marbles out of a container then putting them back in the container, lining up toys a particular way, etc.) and may become dysregulated if their routine is changed in any way. Their need for routine may appear obsessive, and major meltdowns can occur when this routine is modified in any way. Quite often, what neurotypical children view as small problems may be felt as very large problems to a child with ASD.

Other symptoms include flapping, hyperactivity, impulsive behavior, unusual eating and sleeping habits, and difficulties with varying sensory input. A team approach between parents, teachers, mental health therapists, occupational therapists, and other professionals greatly helps these children regulate and feel successful academically, socially, and emotionally.

ANXIETY

Feeling anxiety is a part of life, and therapists will encounter many instances of working with anxious clients no matter the diagnosis. Anxiety disorders are different than this occasional anxiety and will be more persistent, more intense, and of longer duration. There are several different types of anxiety, each with a different set of symptoms; however, the most common symptoms seen under the general heading of "anxiety disorder" are as follows:

Feeling Nervous or on Edge: Children often call this being "stressed," "scared," or "worried." They express feeling out of control and can't fully explain the "why" of this worry. Not understanding why they're feeling anxious often leads to greater anxiety. The anxiety is intense and causes physical reactions, such as a fast heartbeat, sweating, dizziness, and nausea. Children will report feeling their anxiety more days out of the week than not.

Trouble Concentrating: Children with anxiety often have difficulty focusing on their daily routines. They may feel overwhelmed with school work and feel as if they don't know where to start. Even the smallest of tasks may feel overwhelming to them. These children also report feeling forgetful and unable to stop their brains from thinking about their worries.

Trouble Sleeping: Children with anxiety often say that first thing in the morning or right at bedtime are the times when their anxiety is the worst. Due to this, trouble falling asleep is prevalent, as well as staying asleep. Children often report waking up earlier than they need to with a feeling of doom and dread. This lack of sleep can also result in irritability and sleepiness throughout the day.

It has been noted that many children who experience high levels of anxiety are aware of interventions and can fully explain the coping skills they are taught, but the wave of anxiety comes at such a strong level that they have great difficulty trying the interventions when anxiety hits. Teaching these children how to create a calming sensory environment, in addition to completing coping activities as a routine rather than an intervention, can be instrumental in helping to reduce anxiety.

ADHD

ADHD can be diagnosed as primarily the inattentive type, hyperactive/impulsive type, or a combined type. The symptoms of each are summarized below:

Inattentive Type: These children have trouble concentrating and focusing. They may miss small, yet important details when reading or writing. They don't seem to be listening to others and fail to follow through on tasks to completion. These children may be highly disorganized and show poor time management. They may also have executive functioning difficulties.

Hyperactive/Impulsive Type: These children have trouble sitting still and move as if they are constantly "on the go." There will be a great deal of fidgeting and getting up and out of their seats often. They may have difficulty waiting their turn or being quiet when it is expected. Teachers report these children often interrupt others, call out in class, and move around the room at inappropriate times.

The combined type of ADHD will see symptoms in both inattention and hyperactivity/impulsiveness.

One important note: once thought of as primarily a boys' diagnosis, researchers are beginning to note differences between boys and girls with ADHD. Girls with ADHD tend to feel the symptoms more internally and, due to this, also feel more anxiety, social skills deficits, and emotional over-reactivity. The psychologist Kathleen Nadeau has developed a separate screening tool checklist specifically for girls (as of this writing, it can be found at www.additudemag.com/adhd-symptoms-test-girls). This checklist should be a self-report only, since parents and/or teachers may not be aware of the symptoms as girls often hide them from others.

You may notice that despite the differences in symptoms between autism, anxiety, and ADHD, they all have emotion dysregulation in common. Mindfulness interventions can be key to helping all of these children feel more regulated and able to face their challenges with confidence.

Play Therapy
Mindful Interventions

"There needs to be a lot more emphasis on what a child can do rather than what he cannot do."

—Temple Grandin

INTRODUCING PLAY INTO THERAPY

In my play therapy room, I start any new client relationship with non-directive play therapy. My focus in these sessions is on rapport building, and I watch carefully to discover the client's play style, play themes, and any significant verbalizations made. I ensure the client feels safe and secure in the therapy space and follow the lead of the client's play. I am fully present during the session, listening, tracking, and setting limits if needed (limits in this context would be with time and/or safety issues).

Once I believe a healthy rapport has been established, I slowly begin a more directive approach, initially by asking the child what he/she would like to have as a goal for therapy, and what are some current obstacles to this goal. I ensure the client that he/she is the expert of what is needed to reach this goal, and that I am a mentor and a bridge to help in this achievement. The few questions I ask are obviously adapted depending on the age and developmental level of my client, but it is very important for me to have the child's perspective of what is needed before I bring in the parents for treatment planning.

When a solid treatment plan goal has been made with the child's and family's input, I take a hybrid approach in the session, using both non-directive and directive approaches. I begin the session with a brief activity to help with regulation. I assume that all of my clients are dysregulated after a long school day or stress at home, so I always do some type of calming intervention. Examples include brain breaks, yoga poses, or the breathing exercises that are detailed in the following chapter.

After this five-minute activity, I present the client with two or three choices of directive activities I have chosen based on the treatment plan goal (I most definitely do not take a scattered approach to interventions and am very careful to choose interventions that help with the goal!). The client chooses which activity sounds the most interesting, and then we complete together. These interventions typically are no longer than 20 minutes but can always go longer if the client so chooses. The remaining 25 minutes or so of the session is the non-directive time when the client chooses whatever he or she would like to do. Sometimes they wish to continue the directive activity, other times they choose something completely different to do. This structure allows me to ensure that I am working on my clients' goals (which have been agreed upon by both the client and the parents), while still giving clients valuable non-directive time to be free and in control of their play.

All of the interventions in this book have been used during my clients' directive play time. They have been wonderful in promoting mindfulness and regulation, which has led to my clients feeling more confident, more in control, and in better emotional health. A common treatment plan goal is increasing client regulation, which is actualized by reducing meltdowns, promoting awareness, recognizing and verbalizing feelings, etc. These interventions have been useful tools in achieving these goals.

I have organized these play and mindfulness interventions into the following categories:

- Breathing
- Drawing
- Coloring
- Mandala Making
- Nature
- Multi-media
- 3-D
- Movement
- Games
- Storytelling
- Puppet
- Sensory
- Improvisational

Each category contains five to seven interventions for a total of 75 mindful play therapy activities!

Once you begin using these interventions, you will be able to come up with your own variations, and may even discover additional interventions to add to your repertoire. I encourage you to try these on your own first to see for yourself the value of feeling mindful.

A NOTE ABOUT PROCESSING

Processing can be an important piece of additional awareness for the clients, especially those clients who are more verbal in origin. Verbal processing can allow for additional meaning to occur, and the idea that the calmness felt from completing the intervention can be replicated in other settings. This can be an important key towards achieving long-lasting mindfulness, especially considering replication is vital since only achieving calm in the therapy room is not enough.

Processing does not have to be completed after every play therapy intervention. In fact, some more non-directive inclined play therapists do not process at all. There is such intrinsic meaning that occurs during play; to make the assumption that verbal processing needs to occur lessens the value and importance of this play. Verbal processing can also be ineffective for those clients who rely more on bodily awareness, those who are more non-verbal, and those who have language processing difficulties.

In my practice, I always ask the client first if I may ask them some questions about the play therapy intervention we have just completed. I ask this every time, even if the client has previously responded "no" in other sessions. I am most certainly not a mind reader, so I want to make sure the clients have the right after each session to say yes or no to processing. If clients say yes, I ask some very basic questions mostly concerning how they enjoyed the intervention, how they felt in their bodies before/during/after the intervention, and how they could practice this in other settings. Depending on the intervention, I may ask additional questions—mostly focusing on the process of completing the activity. I would never ask processing questions if the client told me "no," and I rarely ask questions during the first few sessions with clients. I want to make sure we have established a solid rapport, so they feel comfortable saying "no" to me if they really don't want to answer any questions.

When my clients complete art-based play therapy interventions, I have specific questions I ask if they are willing to answer. These questions are as follows:

- Would you like to give your work of art a name/title?
- What is happening in this masterpiece?
- I've noticed (point to a particular area, color, or shape). Please tell me more.
- I noticed that you (bodily reactions such as scrunched eyes, hard pressure on marker, tears, sighing, etc.) while creating this part. What do you think about this?
- Looking at your work of art now, do you wonder about any parts of it?
- Let's pretend we could jump into your picture. Let's do it now! (I dramatize this by counting to three and then mimic diving in.) How does it feel to be

in your artwork? What do we notice now that we are in the picture? What do we see/hear/smell/taste/touch?

- Your therapy goal has been _____. How do you think creating this masterpiece may have gotten you closer to your goal?
- What did you learn from creating this work of art?

These questions are from a previous book of mine, *Finding Meaning with Mandalas— A Therapist's Guide to Creating Mandalas with Children* (2015), which focuses on the mandala and its use in interventions with children. However, these questions are applicable to any art-based play therapy intervention.

There is not a one-size-fits-all approach for any therapist working with children. Some therapists feel very comfortable with verbal processing and will enjoy asking questions after play therapy interventions. Other therapists will feel more hesitant and want the focus to be on the play therapy intervention itself. Accept that you, as a therapist, have your own unique and personal style and conduct your play therapy sessions in the way that feels the most genuine to you!

HOW INTERVENTIONS IN THIS BOOK ARE PRESENTED

I wanted to present the interventions in this book in a simple, easy-to-read format. For this reason, I decided to use the following structure:

A brief description of the intervention: I present a brief description to give some ideas on each intervention highlighted in this book.

Materials: This section is in bold print, so you can have materials ready before presenting the intervention to your clients.

Bulleted instructions: Having the directions bulleted will help you more clearly understand how to explain the intervention. The instructions are written as if I am speaking directly to the client. Although this is a reader-friendly way of presenting the directions, please do not feel like this is a script that has to be memorized! It's important to be your genuine self and describe the intervention in your own personal style.

The Pre-Intervention Activity: The Thermometer

Once I have established a rapport with my clients, I introduce the thermometer activity to them. I complete this intervention with every client from the ages of 3 on up. I invite parents into the session for the younger children, so the parents and I can discover together how to best modify it for their child's age and developmental level. I also invite parents to complete the thermometer activity with every member of their family (parents included!) to both normalize the identified child's dysregulation a bit and to learn about every family member's need for calming coping skills.

Another thing I love about this pre-intervention is that we are introducing independence to children. There are times when children can most definitely try to use a coping skill on their own, without having to go to a trusted adult. This activity teaches them when to try a calm down technique on their own and when they need to ask for help. Adults often assume that children know when to be independent and when to ask for help, but this is a skill that needs to be taught.

MATERIALS: Several thermometer templates and a variety of crayons are needed for this pre-intervention.

INSTRUCTIONS:

- Today we are going to really think about your anger (could also be anxiety, distress, etc.). We are going to think about it in three different ways: by color, by number, and by words.

- As you may have heard before, anger has many different levels to it. It may feel like we go from calm to furious, but we really don't. When we become more mindful of how we are feeling in our bodies we can become more successful at taking good care of our anger. *(I do not like using the term "controlling your anger." I like to think of anger, or any other strong emotion, as our friend and teacher that we need to take care of since it can sometimes get us into trouble.)* Today, we are going to discover the different levels of your anger and work on labeling them.

- Please look at this thermometer. What do you know about a thermometer? *(Check to make sure they understand the concept of rising levels in a thermometer representing hotter temperatures! This used to be common knowledge for children, but I've had several clients who do not know what a thermometer is.)*

- Yes! As temperatures get hotter, the color in a thermometer rises to the top. Our anger is the same way. As our anger gets more intense we begin to get "hotter" and more out of control.

- Let's start at the bottom of the thermometer:

  ○ We can call this **Level 1** *(or just "1")*. This is when we are oh so calm! We feel SO good, so carefree, and so chill! Do you remember the time you told me that you felt all warm and fuzzy after getting a hug from your mom? Well, that's an example of Level 1. Now, would you like to write the "1" on the thermometer, or should I? Great!

  ○ Next, let's look at all of these colors we have before us. Which color is your Level 1 color? Which color feels like a Level 1 to you? Please pick one and then color from the Level 1 line down to the bottom of the thermometer.

  ○ Now, let's think about a word or words that remind you of this feeling. I used several earlier, but there may be a word you like better. When you believe you have your perfect Level 1 word, we can write it next to the "1."

  ○ We now have a number, a color, and a word that all goes with this level! Are you ready to move on to the next level?

- *(I then continue this activity in the same manner as explained above, moving from 2 up to 5. I always give descriptive words first, then describe an example of when they expressed feeling this way. They then write the number, choose a color, and choose a word or words.)* Here are some ideas for words at each level:

  ○ **Level 2:** (Just beginning to feel the anger) Irritated, Aggravated, Alarmed, Concerned, Frustrated

- **Level 3:** (Feeling the anger, but still in control) Mad, Pissed *(a common one children choose, so I am okay with it)*, Angry, Irate

- **Level 4:** (More intense and almost at the point of being out of control) Enraged, Really Mad, Extremely Angry, Losing It

- **Level 5:** (The most intense level and, at this point, the client is out of control) Furious, Explosive, Out of Control, Meltdown

- We now have your very own anger thermometer! I am going to talk to your parent about every member in your family creating one of these. It is so important to realize that we all have intense feelings and need to take a break or complete a coping skill when needed.

- Since you all will have different colors or words, as a family you will want to share your numbers with each other since they are the same. Share your numbers often, not just when you're angry! You may start to notice that you are calm more often than you think.

- One more important thing! I need to teach you what to do at each level. We can write this on your thermometer if you would like. At Level 1, do nothing. If we feel calm, there is no need to change it. At Level 2, just pay attention. You don't need to try a coping skill at this point, but notice that you may have to if things don't get better.

- At Level 3, try a coping skill by yourself. You have some great ideas of what you need when angry, and this level is the perfect time to try them on your own. You may be surprised how skilled you are at this!

- At Level 4, get help with a coping skill from one of your trusted people. At this point, you are too close to out of control, so help is needed. At Level 5, well we just may have to accept that we are in meltdown mode and try even harder next time to catch it sooner. With practice, you will notice a lot less Level 5 feelings occurring!

thermometer

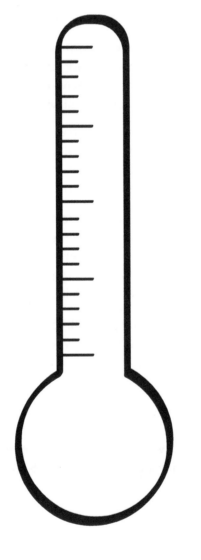

We place the 1, 3, and 5 on the larger lines, and then the children choose on which of the smaller lines the 2 and 4 should go.

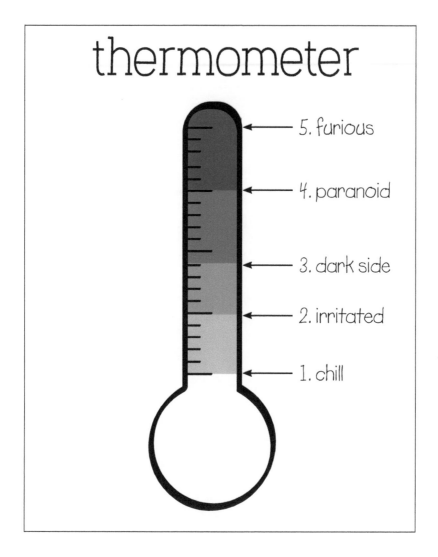

thermometer

5. furious

4. paranoid

3. dark side

2. irritated

1. chill

This is a completed Anger Thermometer from a 20-year-old client with Autism Spectrum Disorder-Level II. I wrote for him due to fine motor difficulties, but he chose the words and colors.

—⑤—
Breathing
Interventions

I have had to become very creative when introducing breathing interventions to my young clients! I suspect this may be due to their learning techniques that they do not find enjoyable or meaningful. I often discover that my clients believe they know breathing techniques, yet when they model them for me, they are not breathing in a mindful way.

When I teach mindful breathing interventions, I have the clients take a longer exhale than inhale to fully experience a calming breath. Researchers have found that when one's exhale is a few seconds longer than the inhale, the vagus nerve sends a signal to the brain, which increases the parasympathetic nervous system. Parasympathetic nervous system increases result in slower breathing, reduced heart rate and blood pressure, and a more relaxed state of calm (Berzin, 2012).

The following breathing interventions are tailored especially for children. I hope you and the youth you are working with will find these practices effective and fun.

Finger Breathing

This exercise is a great way to have children focus on breathing while having the extra sensory component of touch!

MATERIALS: Just your body!

INSTRUCTIONS:

- Hold both hands comfortably on your lap, palms facing up.

- Touch each thumb to index finger, and slowly breathe in through the nose, and blow out through your mouth. Try to blow out a couple of seconds longer than the in-breath.

- Touch each thumb to middle finger and breathe in then out.

- Touch each thumb to ring finger and breathe in then out.

- Touch each thumb to pinky finger and breathe in then out.

- Give your fingers a good STRETCH!

- Repeat the process, but this time go in the opposite order (thumbs to pinky, ring, middle, index).

- Take one more STRETCH, then RELAX!

Cookie Breathing

It's easy to imagine you're cooling off cookies in this fun breathing intervention!

MATERIALS: An image of cookies is needed for this activity.

INSTRUCTIONS:

- Look at all of these different cookie pictures *(a variety can easily be found online)*.

- Pick your favorite, most delicious looking cooking picture.

- Take a deep breath in, smelling the wonderful cookie!

- Take a long blow out, and try to cool down that cookie!

- Repeat three to five times, then RELAX.

Gong Breath

A singing bowl is a wonderful tool for transitions, as well as for this great breathing exercise! It's extra relaxing for children to feel the reverberation of the bowl after striking it. If you don't have a singing bowl, there are free apps you can download with various singing bowl tones!

MATERIALS: A singing bowl or an app with singing bowl tones is needed for this activity.

INSTRUCTIONS:

- Place the singing bowl on a small pillow on the floor.

- Sit cross legged around the singing bowl.

- Strike the singing bowl as hard as you wish.

- Close your eyes, relax, and listen to the tone.

- Hold one finger up when you can no longer hear the bowl.

- Repeat, but this time place your palm one to two inches away from the outside of the bowl—but don't touch the bowl, or the sound will stop!

- Breathe slowly while "feeling" the bowl.

- Hold one finger up when you can no longer feel the bowl.

- Repeat each way one more time for ultimate relaxation!

Mantra Breath

Most children can easily think up a word as their mantra, but having a variety of pictures of faces, places, and things can be helpful for those children who have language difficulties. Have index cards and markers handy to decorate the child's words!

MATERIALS: Pictures of faces, places, and things; index cards; markers or crayons are needed for this intervention.

INSTRUCTIONS:

- Close your eyes.

- Think of something positive you needed to feel or experience this week.

- Quick! Pick the first word that came to your head and share.

- Write your word on the index card, then fill the card however you wish with markers.

- Hold your card, and breathe in slowly.

- Feel the word traveling in you!

- Turn the card over, and quietly blow out any stress onto the blank side. Try to blow out a few seconds longer than you breath in.

- Repeat this three to four times.

Bubble Breathing

This is an oldie but a goodie! Play therapists always have bubbles on hand since they provide such a nice breathing visual.

MATERIALS: Bubbles are needed for this intervention.

INSTRUCTIONS:

- Take the bubble wand out of the bubble container.

- Picture in your head blowing a GIANT bubble.

- Take a soft breath in, trying to capture that image.

- Slowly blow out onto the bubble wand.

- Watch how big of a bubble you can blow!

- Repeat three to four times—or as many times as you need to create the biggest bubble!

— 6 — Drawing Interventions

Drawing is an excellent way to introduce art-based play therapy interventions to clients. Drawing may feel less threatening and easier for the clients to complete. An eraser is all that is needed if the drawing is not going in the direction the client wants it to go!

The simple use of a pencil and paper allows clients to not have to decide upon color choices, which can help them focus more on their inner expressions. Drawing can be a more active activity for clients than coloring a pre-made page, and it requires a degree of planning and challenge.

Clients often have an idea in their heads of what they want to create, then become frustrated when their images don't compare to their ideas. It is for this very reason that I included drawing interventions in this chapter where actual objects are not being drawn. I have found it very beneficial to allow clients to experiment with pencils by scribbling, applying varying amounts of pressure, and creating circles. This cannot only provide relaxation to young clients, but give them the confidence to then tackle more detailed drawing interventions.

Pencil Feelings

Using a pencil allows children to experiment with shading and how lighter vs. more firm pressure feels in their hands. It's a great tool to help children realize how they may hold pressure in their hands when upset and can work on release.

MATERIALS: A nice variety of graphite pencils and paper are needed for this activity.

INSTRUCTIONS:

- Take a sheet of paper and fold it twice to have four spaces.

- Write one feeling on each space.

- Look at the first feeling you chose. Think or talk about a time when you felt this way.

- Choose a graphite pencil and scribble in this space whatever you wish to express this feeling.

- Repeat with the second, third, and fourth feeling.

- When finished, did you notice something different with your scribbles? Were your pleasant feeling scribbles lighter? Darker? Curvier? More jagged?

- When creating, did you notice holding your pencil tighter when creating the unpleasant scribble feelings? Do you think that may happen in your hands when you are experiencing these unpleasant feelings?

- Let's take a nice hand stretch by first clenching our hands and then releasing them. Let's repeat this three times.

- Take your masterpiece home to remind you to STRETCH your hands when unpleasant feelings arrive.

Scribble Drawing

Scribble drawings are such a nice way for children to fully be in the moment with their artwork! Scribbles release any pressure to perform or perfectionism some children may feel when creating, which allows them to focus on the process of drawing rather than the product.

MATERIALS: Multiple sizes of paper, a pencil, crayons, and a one-minute timer are needed for this activity.

INSTRUCTIONS:

- Please choose a paper size that feels the best to you.

- On the count of three, take a pencil and scribble for one full minute until the timer goes off. There is no wrong way to do this!

- Time's up!

- Look at your picture. Do you see any objects in your scribbles? Animals? People? Toys?

- Take your crayons and color in any objects you see in your scribbles. Use your imagination; whatever YOU see is what is real!

- If you like, we can make up a story about your objects, or we can stop at this point and just enjoy your masterpiece!

Circle Picture

Studies have shown that circles are relaxing and symbolize wholeness and the Self. Circle art has been created for centuries by most cultures, and is a wonderful tool for relaxation.

MATERIALS: Paper, pencil, crayons, and circle templates/compass are needed for this activity.

INSTRUCTIONS:

- Take your paper and fill it with as many circles as you wish. Feel free to choose big circles and small circles. You can overlap these circles or keep them separate.

- When you are finished, you may color these circles however you wish, or you can keep them uncolored.

- How did it feel to create circles? Did you know that simply taking a pencil and making circles helps when you're stressed?

- What a great way to get calm no matter where you are!

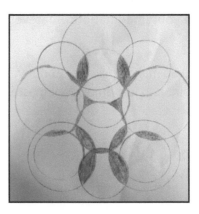

This is an example of a circle drawing titled "Flow" that was created by an adult client.

Draw My

_____

I saw a video entitled *Art as Medicine* in which an art therapist explained the value of "drawing a scream." She explained how no one has ever actually seen a scream, so there is no pressure in creating one! I found this so interesting, so I do this intervention often with children with all kinds of tough emotions. In this scripted intervention, I use ADHD as an example.

MATERIALS: Paper and pencil is all that is needed for this activity.

INSTRUCTIONS:

- You mentioned it's hard to have ADHD. I bet it is! I wonder what having ADHD feels like for you?

- Let's try this. Please take a piece of paper and a pencil. Think about your ADHD. What does it "look" like and feel like to you?

- Draw your ADHD on this paper. Remember, no one has ever "seen" ADHD so there is NO wrong way to do this. However you wish to draw your ADHD is the right way!

- When finished we can talk about it or you can keep your masterpiece to bring home.

Self-Portrait

Having children look in the mirror and then transfer what they see onto paper is a very mindful activity. It is important for them to remember that we are not looking for perfection. Focus on what they see and how they put it on the paper.

MATERIALS: A mirror, paper, and pencil is needed for this activity.

INSTRUCTIONS:

- Many famous artists draw self-portraits. Some of them choose to draw exactly how they see themselves in a mirror. Others like to draw themselves differently, sometimes using shapes or scribbles, or whatever they want. That is the great thing about art!

- Please take the mirror and look at your face. Study it for however long you wish.

- Now, take the pencil and draw on your paper however you'd like to create your own self-portrait masterpiece. Remember, there is NO wrong way to do this. You may use lines, scribbles, shapes, etc.

- When finished you can share your process if you'd like, or just recognize the feelings you felt when creating it.

Faces Fill In

Children enjoy this activity since there are many ways to draw expressions! This can be a great tool to help clients begin to notice how many facial expressions are in play with various emotions! As a special add-in, I also like to practice these expressions on our faces, too.

MATERIALS: A pencil, magazines with a variety of facial expressions, and the Faces Fill In sheet are needed for this intervention.

INSTRUCTIONS:

- We can have so many feelings! Did you know that we can look on people's faces to guess how they are feeling? We can look through this family magazine now to figure out what feelings we notice. Maybe let's just stick with happy, mad, sad, and scared. *(Therapist and client go through magazine looking at various emotions noted on faces. It's important to help process with clients what they are noticing on the faces with different emotions.)*

- What were things you noticed about happy/mad/sad/scared faces? It's interesting how eyebrows, eyes, mouths, and more can look different depending on what feeling they are having, isn't it? Even though not everyone looks the same with each feeling, we definitely noticed some similarities!

- Let's look at the Faces Fill In sheet on the next page. Notice the first circle says "happy" above it. Why don't you take your pencil and draw a happy face inside that circle. Feel free to add in any features you would like. *(Repeat for mad, sad, and scared.)*

- Excellent job creating these feeling faces! What did you notice while creating them? Do the body parts look the same or different with each feeling? How so/how not? Is there a way that we can look at people's faces to help us know how they are feeling? Where are places we can try that?

Faces Fill In

Created by:_____ Date:_____

HAPPY

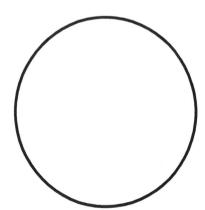

SAD

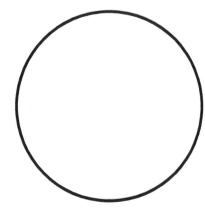

MAD

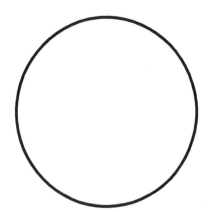

SCARED

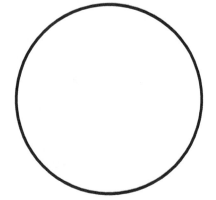

7

Coloring
Interventions

Coloring can be a more passive, and therefore more relaxing, activity for clients. Research has suggested that coloring versus drawing allows for the state of *flow* to occur with participants—*flow* meaning the ability to be fully engaged with the process at hand. This is indeed mindfulness at its best!

Coloring interventions are an easy way to help kids discover mindfulness, and this discovery can lead to even greater moments of focus and calming. The coloring interventions included in this chapter initially focus on fun and self-esteem building, then lead to self-assessment and self-expression.

Color by Number Picture

Coloring can be both fun and freeing when cooperating with another over color choice! This is a great activity to do with families and groups!

MATERIALS: Have a simple mandala printed. The therapist should lightly place a number into each part of the mandala; the number should correspond to the total number of participants. (Example: Four family members participating would have the therapist place a "1," "2," "3," and "4" equally among parts of the mandala.) This activity also needs a bucket of crayons handy.

INSTRUCTIONS:

- Each family member, please pick a crayon color of your choice.

- Each of you are going to be given a number. The youngest family member gets the "1," and the oldest family member gets the "4."

- This is a mandala. Notice how the mandala has numbers on it. Number "1" family member, please color all of the spaces with a "1" inside with your color. *(Continue with the number "2," "3," and "4" family members.)*

- When finished, let's observe the mandala. What are your thoughts? Your observations?

- How did it feel to share in this activity? What do you think about sharing responsibilities? Could this work with other family activities?

- Feel free to take this mandala home as a great reminder of how well you all work together!

Surprise Color Picture

Oftentimes, clients with autism, ADHD, and anxiety have a difficult time in situations where they feel out of control. Practicing not having total control, in a safe and nurturing environment, can be the first step towards more comfort with lack of control in other environments. This is a safe and fun art activity that helps clients begin to feel comfort without total control.

MATERIALS: Have a simple coloring picture (can be found online and chosen by client) and a bucket of crayons.

INSTRUCTIONS:

- We are going to create a very silly picture today! It will be a surprise how it turns out!

- Please pick any object you see in this picture, just one object please. *(For clarity purposes, we will pretend this is a picture of a dog, and the following bullets assume this.)*

- You chose the dog's spots! Please close your eyes and pick a crayon out of the bucket. Whichever color is picked, that is what the spots' colors will be! *(Continue this process with the dog's fur, collar, grass, dog house, etc.)*

- *(When finished)* Wow, look at this picture! How are you surprised? What do you think about this picture? How did it feel to not have control over your colors? How do you feel now looking at it? Are there perhaps other times where you can just be surprised by what happens?

- Please take this picture home as a reminder of how surprises can be silly!

 # Color Chart

This is a well-known play therapy intervention, often done with a heart or rainbow template. It allows therapists to learn which colors clients associate with various emotions. Having an "emotions key" with clients is a great way to later work with them on feelings in their body, using color rather than words. I have also observed that these color identifications do not change over time; my clients' "happy colors" remain the same throughout time. (Not too surprising since, if we think about it, our favorite colors haven't changed!)

MATERIALS: Have the Color Chart template available, as well as a bucket of crayons. I also have a feeling chart handy for the clients to choose two additional feelings.

INSTRUCTIONS:

- Did you know that different colors remind us of different feelings? It's true! Each of us have personal preferences for colors, viewing some as happy others as sad. The great thing about this is that there is no wrong happy or sad color—it's up to us to decide what feels right!

- Let's think about the word "happy." What do you think happy means? What reminds you of happy? How does it feel in your body when you're happy? Now pick the crayon that feels the most like your happy feeling, and color in the happy box. *(Follow this same process for sad, mad, and scared.)*

- We have room for two more feelings. What is a feeling you often have that we didn't talk about? Feel free to look at this chart for help. *(Once chosen, follow the same script. Repeat for the second feeling.)*

- Look at your feeling chart! We now know your emotion colors! If you'd like, you could take this home or we can keep it in your file. *(I like to have an additional copy of this in the client's file in order to complete The Colors in Me intervention.)*

| _____'S Color Chart |

Date:_____

HAPPY

SCARED

SAD

MAD

The Colors in Me

The Colors in Me is a follow-up activity to the Color Chart intervention. This intervention helps clients mindfully discover which feelings are within them at various times. I often give extra body templates to the children's parents as an extension for home. I will also ask clients throughout the session which colors are in them to determine current feelings without having to complete the coloring activity.

MATERIALS: The Colors in Me template and the specific crayons chosen by the client for the Color Chart activity are needed for this exercise.

INSTRUCTIONS:

- Let's take a look at this template. It shows all parts of our body. We can think about what is on the outside or on the inside of our bodies while completing this activity.

- Let's first do one of the breathing activities so we can feel calmer. *(I allow client to choose breathing activity.)*

- Aahhh… Now that we are calmer, let's close our eyes and try to "sense feel" our body. *(I have taught my clients that "sense feels" are sensations, pressures, feelings, etc., that we have in our body.)* What are you noticing? Any pressure? Any pain? Any flutters? Any warmth? Any coolness?

- Now, let's look at your happy, sad, mad, scared, _____, and _____ crayons. *(The last two feelings depend on what the client chose when completing the Color Chart.)*

- Can you show me on this picture where you are feeling these feelings in your body?

- Feel free to color on this body whatever feelings you are experiencing in your body.

- If you are feeling pain, what feeling goes with pain for you? If you are feeling squiggly, what feeling goes with that? *(You can talk clients through this if necessary.)*

- Let's take a look at what you've created. Tell me about these feelings in your body. Is there anything we can do in here to lessen or strengthen any of these feelings?

- Let's make sure you take some of these templates home, so you can work on this whenever you are unsure of your feelings.

The Colors in Me

Date: _____

Front   Back

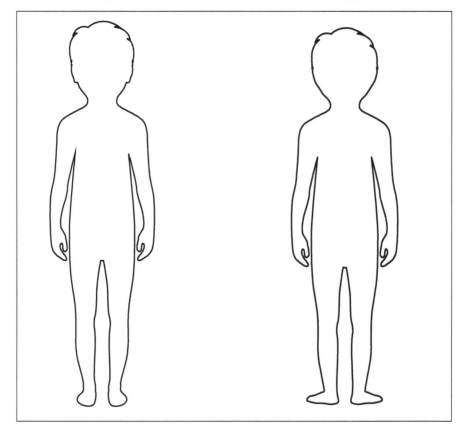

Use your feelings crayons to show
what you are feeling throughout your body.

Color My Mood

I am a fan of abstract art. I believe it can be freeing for clients who are often concerned with control, perfectionism, or understanding directions. I like to show clients some examples of abstract art prior to an activity to discuss the artwork and the feelings it evokes. It's amazing to me how clients can discuss how they feel from the color, intensity, and shapes within a work of art! This activity allows them to be their own artist and create their own mood work of art. It is similar to the Scribble Art activity, except this is a bit more directive since we are asking clients to focus on their current mood. We are also using color in this activity.

A quick note: I do NOT limit clients to their "emotion crayons" discovered during the Color Chart activity. I have a full bucket of crayons from which to choose!

MATERIALS: Blank paper and a bucket of crayons are needed for this activity.

INSTRUCTIONS:

- Do you remember when we looked at abstract art? You were able to recognize so many feelings and emotions from the pictures we viewed! I believe that we can all be great artists and create art from whatever mood we are feeling.

- Let's first do one of the breathing activities so we can feel calmer. *(I allow client to choose breathing activity.)*

- Aahhh… That feels good. Now let's think about our mood. *(I use the word "mood" to describe temporary feelings that we are having in our body. Have clients focus on the fact that moods can switch often, even during the therapy session!)*

- What feelings are we noticing in our bodies? If we close our eyes, which colors are we seeing? *(Give clients a chance to mentally observe.)*

- Please take this piece of paper and create your own masterpiece. Use whatever colors you wish to create any marks, shapes, lines, squiggles, etc. you need to show your mood masterpiece.

- Don't forget there is no wrong way to do this, and don't think too hard! Allow your hand to do the moving in whatever way it needs to!

- When finished, please feel free to discuss your masterpiece if you wish. Would you give it a title?

- How would you describe this work of art?

- How did it feel creating it?

- Please feel free to take your mood masterpiece home.

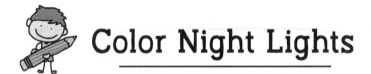

Color Night Lights

I have several clients who have difficulty falling asleep. Many of them have vivid imaginations and get scared at night. I have found that first completing a breathing exercise, and then creating these colorful night lights to take home, has really helped them feel calmer in their bedrooms.

MATERIALS: A sheet of tracing paper, a variety of crayons, clear tape, and a flameless LED tea light (which can be bought cheaply in bulk at most craft stores).

INSTRUCTIONS:

- I remember you telling me how difficult it is for you to fall asleep at night. Sometimes our imaginations go into overdrive in our bedrooms, and we get afraid to fall asleep.

- It helps when we have something calming in our room to look at. It can be extra special when it's something that we have created ourselves. Would you like to create a special calming object to help you sleep?

- Let's first complete one of our breathing exercises to make sure we are nice and calm. Which one would you like to do? *(Complete the exercise with the child.)*

- Aahhh… Now we feel nice and calm! What are some people, places, things, colors, and shapes that help you feel calm? What nice objects you've named!

- Now, let's take this piece of tracing paper and this bucket of crayons. Notice how this paper is thinner than a typical sheet of paper. When you color on tracing paper you will need to be gentler with your crayon.

- I would like for you to color in this piece of paper however you wish. You may make an abstract picture or a detailed picture. You may use shapes, colors, and symbols of your choice to fill it in however you would like. There is no wrong way to do this!

- Exquisite! Now, I will help you tape the short edges together to make it look like a cylinder.

- We can now switch on this LED tea light, then place your artwork over it. Do you see how it glows?

- Your beautiful masterpiece has become a night light! Do you know where you can place this in your bedroom?

- Could you practice one of our breathing activities before bed, and then turn this on?

- I wonder if this will help you get a great night's sleep?

8

Mandala Interventions

I have discovered so much healing and growth can occur through creating mandalas that I wrote a book on them! In *Finding Meaning with Mandalas: A Therapist's Guide to Creating Mandalas with Children* (2015), I detailed 50 mandala interventions that can be created by children to help build mindfulness and self-regulation skills. I chose the seven most popular mandala creations (based on my clients) to include in this book.

In case you are asking, "What is a mandala?" the word mandala simply means "circle" in Sanskrit. Creating mandalas have been prevalent in many cultures for thousands of years. Research has shown that when children create art within a circle, it can have healing properties and can help clients feel less resistant towards creating art.

The instructions for each of these mandalas are briefer than what I typically do with my clients. I often conduct mandala sessions where I prepare the room and the materials, introduce the session, and then have a specific way of processing the mandala. Even though these directions are brief, they are a great introduction to using mandalas in therapy sessions with children.

Non-Directive Mandala

Non-directive mandalas give clients free expression towards creating whatever they wish in their special circle. It can be challenging for some clients who are hesitant or doubtful of their artistic ability. For this reason, I offer many different sizes of mandala templates, allowing the clients to choose the least threatening size for their creation. The size of a template can be a definite factor in the confidence level of the children!

MATERIALS: White paper circles of various sizes, pencil, crayons, markers, pastels, etc. are needed for this activity.

INSTRUCTIONS:

- Please take whichever size circle you wish for your mandala work of art.

- Typically, artists look to the center of a mandala to start. They choose a shape, symbol, picture, or word to put in the center. From there, they work their way out, filling the mandala with color, symbols, and shapes of their choosing.

- Please fill your mandala however you wish. You can use any color or design, and please remember there is no wrong way of creating a mandala!

- I will be quiet while you are creating, and you can choose to listen to relaxing music if that makes you feel more comfortable. You let me know when you are finished. *(I have a singing bowl they can strike when finished, but that is not necessary. The important part is making sure the clients decide when they are finished and that we aren't interrupting their process by asking, "Are you finished?")*

- Now that you are finished, talk to me about your creation! Would you give it a title?

- How did it feel when creating it?

- Were you aware of anything else when creating this masterpiece?

- If not, this is mindfulness! What are other ways you can find mindfulness?

- You may take this mandala home to help you remember your feelings when creating your mandala.

Non-directive mandala created by a 12-year-old
client titled "Floral Art."

One-Color Mandala

Creating one-color mandalas is a wonderful tool for helping clients narrow down their creations to the art of creating. Oftentimes, children get very caught up in which colors they want their artwork to be and become anxious trying to decide on color themes. In this activity, the clients can use many shades of just one color, which seems to help with indecision. Focusing on one color also seems to help the client more fully identify with feelings they experience when creating. I've often noticed they associate feelings with particular colors (as also noticed with the Color Chart, The Colors in Me, and Color My Mood interventions), and the color they choose for this activity often corresponds with their current mood.

MATERIALS: Cardboard circle templates (or paper plates) and individual gallon bags with multiple shades of the eight main colors (red, yellow, orange, green, blue, purple, brown, and black) are needed for this activity. My individual bags contain colored pencils, crayons, permanent markers, and pastels, which is why I don't use a paper template.

INSTRUCTIONS:

- Please look at all of these bags of colors and choose the bag of colors that feels right to you.

- Take your mandala template and fill it with any shapes, symbols, words, or pictures you want, only using the shades of color from the bag you chose.

- Remember that there is no wrong way to do this! It helps to start in the center of the circle with a shape, symbol, word, or picture, and then move outwards.

- I will be quiet while you are creating, and you can choose to listen to relaxing music if that makes you feel more comfortable. You let me know when you are finished.

- Now that you are finished, talk to me about your creation! Would you give it a title?

- How did it feel when creating it?

- Were you aware of anything else when creating this masterpiece?

- If not, this is mindfulness! What are other ways you can find mindfulness?

- You may take this mandala home to help you remember your feelings when creating your mandala.

Gem Mandala

Gem mandalas allow children to use a different medium for mandala creation, while still allowing for mindfulness and self-discovery. Many clients may not enjoy coloring or may have fine motor difficulties, which makes them somewhat resistant towards creating art. Using sticky gems to create a mandala is less threatening, while still beautiful and the client's creation. It can be a wonderful bridge towards later creating with other more intimidating mediums.

An important note! Only have available the number of gems you are comfortable with your client using! If you have 5,000 gems out, clients may actually use every single one of them! I have found around 50 to 75 gems is a nice number for mandala creation.

MATERIALS: Circular paper plates, self-adhesive gems, and markers are needed for this activity.

INSTRUCTIONS:

- Have you ever seen stained glass windows? If not, we can look at a few on the computer. These are beautiful works of art using a special glass technique to make the different colors.

- We can make a mandala that looks shiny and colorful, similar to a stained-glass window! You will still be the artist but will not need to use crayons and markers for this mandala.

- Please take this paper plate and look at all of the gems. Pick the gem you feel is the best to place in the center of the plate.

- Now fill the mandala with as many gems as you wish. There is no wrong way to do this! You can use as few or as many of the gems that are here!

- I will be quiet while you are creating, and you can choose to listen to relaxing music if that makes you feel more comfortable. You let me know when you are finished.

- Now that you are finished, talk to me about your creation! Would you give it a title?

- How did it feel when creating it?

- Were you aware of anything else when creating this masterpiece?

- If not, this is mindfulness! What are other ways you can find mindfulness?

- You may take this mandala home to help you remember your feelings when creating your mandala.

Coffee Filter Mandala

It is so enjoyable to watch children's reactions with this activity! It can also be a meaningful metaphor of how change can be both unexpected and beautiful. There can be a great deal of discussion into this concept after the mandala is completed. This is another mandala that is less intimidating for clients who do not feel they are good at art because they know that their scribbles will be transformed with the water spray!

MATERIALS: A coffee filter, washable markers, a spray bottle filled with water, a piece of cardstock, a plastic tablecloth, and paper towels for clean-up are needed for this intervention.

INSTRUCTIONS:

- This activity allows us to be surprised by what you are creating! Your art is going to morph into another masterpiece!

- Please notice we have this coffee filter on a piece of cardstock, which is on top of a plastic tablecloth. This is because the coffee filter will be getting wet!

- You are going to color this coffee filter with these washable markers. You can fill the coffee filter as full as you want with your choice of colors.

- There is no wrong way to do this! In fact, scribbling is encouraged in this activity since the artwork will change!

- When finished, I will hand you this spray bottle, and you are going to spray water onto your masterpiece. One spray at a time will allow you to watch your artwork morph into another beautiful work of art!

- Remember, water can always be added but not taken away! It's better to do one spray at a time, and then you can decide when your masterpiece is complete.

- When completed, we can let it dry; and then, if you'd like, we can tape this onto a piece of construction paper to make it sturdier, or you can choose to keep it as is.

- Now that you are finished, talk to me about your creation! Would you give it a title?

- How did it feel when creating it?

- How did you notice your masterpiece changing while you were spraying it?

- How did you feel about this change?

- Are there other changes in your life that you may be able to compare to this activity?

- You may take this mandala home to help you remember your feelings when creating your mandala.

Stone Mandala

I particularly enjoy creating interventions when cheap and easy-to-find materials are needed. I fully realize that not all who read this book will have dedicated play therapy rooms, and the cost of materials alone can have therapists running from interventions! What could be easier than collecting some stones on your next walk—or even collecting stones on one of the activity walks I discuss later in this book?

MATERIALS: Stones of various sizes and shapes and a white tablecloth are needed for this activity. A permanent marker may be needed if choosing to create a mantra stone for the child.

INSTRUCTIONS:

- Notice the many stones I have here on this tablecloth. They all are different sizes and shapes, just like all of us!

- You will be creating a stone mandala with as many stones as you want. First, please choose your first stone. This will be the center stone. Choose whichever stone feels right to you, and place in the center of the tablecloth.

- Now you can choose some more stones to go around this center stone. You can use as many or as few stones as you like. You can make a closed, tight circle around your center stone or a loose open circle. There is no wrong way to do this!

- Now, take a look at your creation. How would you like to add your third ring? Maybe with a tighter/looser/closer or farther ring of stones? Maybe using smaller or larger stones? The choice is up to you!

- Now that you have created three rings, you can choose if you'd like to continue or keep your masterpiece as is. You may also choose to fill in your mandala with other stones among the rings.

- Let's take a picture of your mandala so you can remember it! *(This mandala obviously can't be taken home, so the idea of impermanence may need to be processed as well.)* Although you cannot take the entire mandala home, how about your special middle stone?

- If you like, you can write a word, a symbol, a shape, or whatever you wish with this permanent marker on your center stone.

- How did you feel before/during/after creating this masterpiece?

- How do you feel about it having to be taken apart?

- Have you felt this feeling before when something has to change?

Candy Mandala

I have found that the simple act of sharing food in sessions can be such a connecting activity! We do have to be mindful of clients' allergies and sensitivities, so having this question on intake forms is highly valuable. This intervention can also be done with fruit, vegetables, and grains, which can be as colorful as candy. The interesting thing about clients creating candy mandalas is that they tend to not want to eat it after they are finished!

MATERIALS: A variety of colorful candies; a large, circular paper plate; and a gallon sized plastic bag are needed for this activity. Fresh fruits, vegetables, and grains may also be used.

INSTRUCTIONS:

- Look at all of this candy! What do you think about this? Today you are going to create a masterpiece using candy instead of paint or markers!

- Please take this paper plate, then look at all of the candy in front of you. Which piece of candy feels right for you to be the center of your artwork? Take your time picking the special center.

- Now, feel free to use additional candies to fill your paper plate however you wish. There is no wrong way to do this! Take your time and let me know when you are finished.

- Now that you are finished, how did it feel to create a candy masterpiece? Did you notice anything sensory going on with you? *(Many report loving the smell of candy or not liking the stickiness of it.)* How did you cope with this extra sensory effect? Was it hard to not eat the candy? Why or why not?

- Let's take a picture of your mandala so you can take it home. You, of course, can take the mandala home in this plastic bag, but know that it won't stay exactly as you have it now.

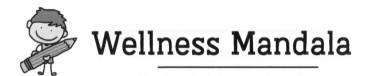

Wellness Mandala

Wellness Wheels are often done with adult clients to assess their current levels of health and balance. They can be an excellent tool to not only see the areas of wellness that need attention, but those areas of wellness that are full. This helps clients see the positive aspects of their current situations. In this activity, children are able to create their own wellness mandalas using a similar technique as the Wellness Wheel. I tend to use this with my clients over the age of 10, but I have had younger clients be able to fully participate in this intervention.

MATERIALS: A pre-drawn segmented circle template, pencil, bucket of crayons, and the Types of Health sheet are needed for this activity. I read the Types of Health sheet to the children, but they could also read it themselves if they so choose.

INSTRUCTIONS:

- We have different types of wellness and health; can you think of some? *(Typically, "physical" is named quickly, but children may need help coming up with others.)*

- It's important for us to check in with ourselves often to see how we are doing in all areas of our health. We may be eating healthy, which is great, but not getting enough sleep! We may be having a great time with our friends, but not completing our homework. Our goal is to try to be as balanced in health as we can and to work on those areas of health that are weaker.

- Please take this circle while I read first about Physical Health. Which segment of your circle would you like to be physical? Please write "physical" on that segment.

- Now, listen as I read to you a couple of questions about physical health. Think about your own physical health as I read.

- Please choose a color that feels like physical health to you. How full do you believe your physical health is at this time? Starting from the center of the circle and moving out shows the degree of no physical health to full physical health. This means if you colored the entire segment of Physical Health, then you believe you are in the best physical health possible! Most of us don't feel we are in the worst or best of any of our health, so find a spot within those two points.

- Once you've decided where your physical health is, take your crayon and draw a line horizontally (across) the Physical Health segment. Then color from the line down to the center of the circle.

- *(Repeat these directions for Emotional, Mental, Spiritual, Social, Financial, Family, and Intellectual Health.)*

- Now, let's look at your Wellness Mandala. Where are you full?

- Where are you empty?

- What have you discovered by completing this activity?

- Are there any changes you can make to help some areas be fuller?

- Is there anything I can do to help you become fuller?

- Please take this mandala home so you can look at it and focus on your goal. We can do another one in a few months to see how you've progressed.

Types of Health

Physical: Am I eating well, sleeping enough, exercising, and balancing my school/work versus my leisure time?

Emotional: Am I taking care of, expressing, and acknowledging my feelings—not trying to run from my feelings nor become too entrenched in them?

Mental: Am I making wise choices, weighing out all options and focusing on my needs? Am I able to think clearly and rationally?

Spiritual: Have I been active in my church/mosque/temple, or spent time praying/meditating/being in nature?

Social: Have I been balancing my social life—not spending too much or too little time with my friends?

Financial: Have I had extra money to treat myself, either through my allowance or my job?

Family: Have I been able to spend fun, quality time with my family? Has my family been nurturing and supportive to each other?

Intellectual: Have I been spending enough time on my school studies or other intellectual pursuits?

WELLNESS MANDALA

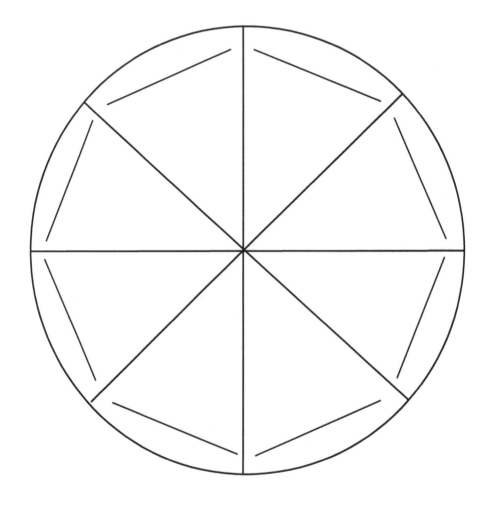

9

Nature Interventions

I am fortunate to have my office in a location where we can go directly outside and experience nature. Because of this, nature interventions have become a regular part of the interventions I create with clients. If this is not possible for you, there are ways you can bring nature to your clients.

Having a therapy room with a variety of natural objects, such as leaves, pebbles, moss, etc., can promote the idea of using pieces of nature in therapeutic interventions. It could also be wonderful to teach the clients' parents specific ways to walk mindfully outdoors so the entire family can experience mindful nature interventions!

Nature Walk

For many children (and adults), there are few things as relaxing as a walk. The best walks are those that have no destination, no time frame, and no hurry. Nature walks are the first walks I introduce to my child clients to in order to get them acquainted with the feeling of wandering.

MATERIALS: A paper bag is all that is needed for this activity.

INSTRUCTIONS:

- Today is a perfect day for a nature walk! Have you ever taken one before? There aren't many rules to a nature walk; we basically walk and discover nature!

- There are some safety rules we must discuss first. *(These can include staying by the therapist, staying on the sidewalk, holding the therapist's hand, etc.)*

- There is also an important nature rule. We can only collect nature that is not on someone's property or nature that has already fallen off of a bush/tree. We don't want to "steal" nature or pick living nature!

- If you're ready, please take a paper bag, and I will take one too. While we're walking slowly, we will pick up any nature that feels good to us and put it in our paper bag. We will together decide when to return.

- Once we return, we pool our nature and decide what to do with it. *(See the Nature Picture activity on the next page for further instructions.)*

Nature Picture

This activity can easily be done after the Nature Walk described earlier. The idea came from a client who wanted a way to work with the beautiful pieces of nature he found. We are lucky in the Midwest to have four distinct seasons, which allows for four very different and surprising nature walks and pictures each year! However, no matter where you live, using "baby eyes" when walking can allow you to see new nature all of the time!

MATERIALS: The bag of nature from the walk, a white plastic tablecloth, paper, glue and/or tape, contact paper, and crayons are the materials needed for this activity.

INSTRUCTIONS:

- Now that we have returned from our Nature Walk, let's place all of our nature onto this tablecloth. What wonderful treasures we have found!

- Let's think about what type of nature picture you can create. Do you think you will be able to fit all of your nature onto this page or only some? Do you think you will keep your nature as is or change it in some way? What ideas are you thinking you may do?

- Please take this paper and first just experiment with your nature. Place it on the paper however you choose. Move it around and try multiple ways of placing. Continue doing this until it all feels just right.

- Now please take the glue and/or tape and create your Nature Picture. Feel free to add your own drawing/coloring if you wish. It is your masterpiece and you may complete it in whatever way feels right to you!

- Now that you are finished, let's discuss your beautiful masterpiece. Would you give it a title? Describe the picture. If we both could "jump" in the picture what would it be like?

- Before we are complete, we should wrap this picture in contact paper to keep the nature safe and on your paper. This may also help the nature stay the colors it currently is. Then you can take it home and have a lasting memory of our Nature Walk!

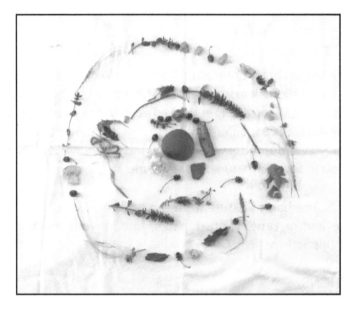

Nature Picture created by 12-year-old client. This was made smaller to fit on an 8 x 11 inch piece of cardstock, and the center stone was replaced with the client coloring a picture of a black stone.

Baby Eyes Walk

In his book *The Miracle of Mindfulness: An Introduction to the Practice of Meditation,* Vietnamese Buddhist monk Nhat Hanh explains the concept of a beginner's mind walk:

> *People usually consider walking on water or in thin air a miracle. But I think the real miracle is not to walk either on water or in thin air, but to walk on earth. Every day we are engaged in a miracle which we don't even recognize: a blue sky, white clouds, green leaves, the black, curious eyes of a child—our own two eyes. All is a miracle.* (Nhat Hanh, 1999)

When reading this book, and especially this quote, I realized that taking beginner's mind walks with my clients could definitely help with self-regulation and awareness! I began introducing Baby Eyes walks to my clients, and they were highly receptive to them! These walks are requested often, and, like all of the walks highlighted in this book, it can easily be replicated in a variety of settings.

INSTRUCTIONS:

- What have you noticed about babies? Have you ever noticed how excited they get with the simplest of things? It seems like they discover new things all of the time!

- Do you think we notice new things or do you think we may walk around life not really paying attention? I sometimes take walks with my dogs around the block, and I'm not sure I'm even paying attention!

- Today we are going to take a special walk. It's called a Baby Eyes walk! Luckily, we don't have baby legs, so we can actually go on this walk! We are just pretending that our eyes are like a baby's eyes.

- How do you think our eyes can be like a baby's eyes? That's right, when we pay attention to what is out there instead of just walking without noticing! Let's do just that!

- So, we are going to walk around the block *(something typically done during therapy sessions to regulate)*, but THIS time we are going to walk with baby eyes. Let's see what we notice! I bet we see things we've never seen before. Let's go!

- Now that we have returned, what did you notice about this Baby Eyes walk?

- Was it more or less peaceful than usual walks?

- More or less enjoyable?

- Why do you think that is?

- Do you think there are other times and places where a Baby Eyes walk could help you?

- When and where?

Sensory Walk

Sensory walks are a wonderful way to practice mindful walking through using your senses. Focusing on one sense of the child's choosing creates a calm abiding and allows for a peaceful walk. This activity can be easily replicated at home or school whenever children need to regulate.

INSTRUCTIONS:

- Today we are going to take a sensory walk! It is different than a regular walk. During this walk we are going to practice paying attention primarily to one of our senses.

- Which sense would you like to focus on? Would you like to focus on what we see, hear, smell, touch, or taste on our walk? Anything you choose sounds great to me!

- Now that you've chosen to focus on seeing/hearing/smelling/touching/tasting on this walk, we are now ready. While on our walk, each of us can call out different sights/sounds/smells/feelings/tastes we are experiencing. Both of us can try to focus on whatever is called out. Only one of us may experience a sensory object and that is okay, too! We are going to work hard at being "sensory detectives" to seek out any sights/sounds/smells/feelings/tastes that are out there. Let's go!

- Now that we are back, let's review what we experienced. About how many sights/sounds/smells/smells/feelings/tastes did we have? Do you think this is more or less than what we typically experience? Why do you think that is?

- Do you think there are other times and places where a Sensory Walk could help you? Let's talk about that!

 # Leaf Art

As children, making leaf rubbing pictures was one of my sister's and my favorite art activities! I was surprised with how many of my clients have never heard of this intervention! Leaf art is definitely a multi-sensory experience with children being able to see, smell, and touch the leaf, and then rhythmically rubbing the crayon against the paper. In addition, this is a "non-knowing" art activity, where often the finished product looks different than they imagined! I find this type of art such a wonderful metaphor for the inconsistency of life!

MATERIALS: Various leaves, two pieces of thin paper, tape, and oil pastels are needed for this activity.

INSTRUCTIONS:

- Today we are going to make some leaf art! Let's first go outside and collect some leaves. We will only need about five leaves total, since we will be placing them on this sheet of paper. *(You can always have leaves ready ahead of time, but have plenty if you do so that the client ultimately chooses his/her favorites.)*

- Now that we've returned, please take this piece of paper and place the leaves on it in whatever design you want. **Make sure you place the leaves vein side up!**

- Once they are placed exactly how you like, let's tape them down a bit so they will be sturdier. *(I modified this activity by doing this since we were having a lot of frustration with moving leaves!)*

- Now, let's place this sheet of paper carefully on top of the leaves.

- Next, please take any oil pastels you wish and gently color onto the paper. You can use as many or as few pastels as you want—it's your choice! *(I have one box of my pastels individually unwrapped for this activity. I have found my clients find it very soothing to lay the pastel flat, and design by moving the pastel back and forth.)*

- Now that you are finished, let's pick up the paper and look at your masterpiece! What do you think? Is it what you expected? How so or how not?

- Can you think of other times in your life when things have turned out better or worse than you thought?

- How did you deal with it?

- Could this beautiful work of art remind you of how things can be different than you think but still okay?

 # Cloud Watching

This is yet another intervention that my generation did often as children, yet many children today have never heard of it! It is a simple way to be out in nature with your clients, being both creative and mindful. If you have windows in your office, it can even be done inside, although being outside in nature is always ideal!

MATERIALS: No materials are needed for this intervention, except for a day that has clouds!

INSTRUCTIONS:

- When I was a child, we would lay down in the grass and look up at the clouds. We would spend a lot of time looking at individual cloud shapes and describing what they look like. It's a really relaxing way to enjoy being outdoors and to calm our brains.

- Let's try this together! We can go outside and sit on the porch, or take a walk and look up at the sky.

- Now that we are looking, pick a cloud! It can be any cloud you choose. What does it look like? Describe it to me. If it had a smell/sound/taste/texture, what would it be?

- Let's continue on and choose more clouds! How fun it is to see the different shapes and pretend they also have sounds/smells/tastes/textures!

10

Multi-Media Interventions

Multi-media artwork can provide just the right touch of mindfulness to any intervention. Many clients may have fine motor difficulties, which cause some difficulty when attempting to draw or color. Multi-media materials allow clients to experience art in a way that allows them to feel successful and competent in their work.

Multi-media interventions can also be a great introduction for perfectionistic clients who become dysregulated when their drawings do not turn out exactly the way they wanted them. Once clients experience success with multi-media art, they may be more inclined to try art interventions that may be more challenging for them.

Feelings Collage

Magazine pictures and postcards can work as great art tools, especially with children who are not confident with their artistic abilities. My favorite magazines have lots of pictures of families, animals, and travel locations. Creating collages is not only a mindful activity, but can also be a bridge towards building clients' artistic confidence.

MATERIALS: One sheet of paper, various magazines, postcards, scissors, glue, and markers are needed for this activity.

INSTRUCTIONS:

- We all have a lot of feelings. What are some of the feelings you feel the most?

- Today you are going to be able to make a feelings collage. Think about which feeling you would like to focus on for this art activity. Which one sounds best to you?

- Now you can look through these magazines and postcards. Look for images that remind you of that feeling. You can choose any image you like—it only needs to make sense to you! When you find images that fit your feeling, you can tear or cut out those images.

- Once you have found all of your images, start arranging them on your paper. Let's not glue them yet so you can really experiment with where you want all of the images. Take your time on this!

- Now that you have decided how to arrange your images, you can glue them onto your page. You can also use markers to decorate your collage however you wish.

- Wow, look at your masterpiece! Would you like to give it a title?

- Describe your artwork to me. What did you notice when searching for images/arranging the images/gluing the images?

- Talk to me about what your images mean (the chosen feeling) to you.

Feelings Collage created by 10-year-old client
titled "Love Feelings."

Strength Cape

I was at a Play Therapy training where the topic was superheroes. At this training, I learned an easy way to make a cape from a white t-shirt. My clients seem to love superheroes, and the metaphor of superheroes having both strength and flaws is relatable to all of us. Rather than create superhero capes with my clients, I decided to name them Strength Capes, where we can focus on individual gifts and strengths.

MATERIALS: A white t-shirt pre-cut into a cape, cardboard (to put underneath the cape to prevent bleeding of colors), and fabric markers are needed for this intervention. (I like to buy X-Large children's size, so every child's head will fit through the neck hole.)

HOW TO CUT A T-SHIRT INTO A CAPE:

1. Lay the shirt flat, front side facing up.

2. Cut off the sleeves at the seams.

3. Cut off each of the side seams.

4. Open up the shirt and cut off the entire front of the shirt; leave the neck hole intact.

INSTRUCTIONS:

- Tell me about your favorite superhero. What are some of his/her strengths?

- Did you notice that superheroes have challenges too? Just like all of us, even superheroes have to work on their difficulties. Superheroes learn how to focus on their strengths, so they can work through their weaknesses.

- Let's think about your strengths—your special gifts that make you, YOU! What are some of them? *(For clients who have difficulty naming strengths, I ask "What would your mom/dad/sister/brother/ friend/teacher, etc. say your strengths are? Do you agree?" This helps them come up with strengths much easier.)*

- Here is your very own cape! It is a very special cape; it will be your strength cape! You can wear it whenever you want, maybe when you need reminding of how special you are!

- Feel free to decorate this cape however you wish with these fabric markers. There is no wrong way to do this! Fill up this cape with any words, symbols, letters, shapes, or images that feel right to you.

- Now that you're finished, what do you think?

- What do you think about your strength cape?

- Describe your images.

- How did it feel creating these images on your cape?

- Can you think of times you can wear this cape to help you remember how strong you are?

Sweet Dreams Shirt

Many of my clients have sleeping issues. Most of these issues can be resolved with sleep schedules and setting the mood for sleep (turning down lights, applying lotion, no electronics, etc.). I have also found that creating a sweet dreams shirt during the session seems to help them remember all we discussed in the session. They all seem to love looking at the artwork they created on the shirt!

MATERIALS: An XL white t-shirt, cardboard, and fabric markers are needed for this activity.

INSTRUCTIONS:

- Sleeping can be difficult, can't it? What are some of the tricks you use for setting the mood for sleep? *(If none have been tried, I may skip this intervention and instead work on a sensory routine for bedtime. The Sweet Dreams Shirt activity would then be completed at the next session.)*

- Did you know people love to have blankets on them even if it is hot outside? Blankets provide comfort and help us feel all snug and cozy. When we're cozy we usually can go right to sleep and have sweet dreams.

- What would sweet dreams look like to you? *(Allow for lots of processing ideas of pictures, places, colors, etc., that would make sweet dreams for the client.)*

- Why don't you create a sweet dreams shirt that you can wear every night at bedtime? You can use this shirt and these fabric markers to design it however you want! You could use what you discussed about sweet dreams and design symbols, shapes, colors, and pictures to represent them.

- Make sure you put the cardboard inside the shirt, so the colors don't run onto the back. Feel free to create your shirt however you wish!

- When finished, you can take this shirt home and wear it at night to help you remember all the sweet dreams you can have, feeling warm and cozy in your new sweet dreams shirt!

 # Paint Mixing

This activity is *so* relaxing, and I would have never thought about it without a client introducing me to it! I have a pre-teen client on the autism spectrum who once asked me if he could use my tempera paints. I, of course, said yes and pulled out the paints for him to use. He then asked if he could have six paper plates (we use these for palettes) and six brushes. I obliged, not knowing what he was going to do with them, and then asked what type of canvas he wanted to use. When he replied "none," I decided to just go ahead and go with whatever his plan was! He carefully chose two or three colors at a time, squirted some of each onto the palette, and used a brush to mix them.

I could see him visibly calming while doing this! He repeated five more times until he had six interesting colors in front of him. He explained how paint mixing relaxed him and he wasn't sure why.

We processed how it was most likely a sensory experience for him: looking at the new color being created, hearing the sound of the brush swirling the paint, smelling the slight scent of the tempera paint, and the gentle circular motion of mixing. He readily agreed! He asked if I thought it was wasteful that he didn't want to actually paint with the new colors and I said absolutely not! How could a child experiencing such regulation be wasteful?

I have repeated this activity with many other clients, starting with just one paper plate, two paint colors, and one brush. I monitor how much they squeeze out (and my particular paint bottles are ideal to limit how much paint is being used!). I then ask if they would like to create another paint color, and we continue until they feel relaxed. Some clients want to create a picture with their new colors, some feel the mixing is enough. Regardless, the regulation and mindfulness they experience just by the act of paint mixing is wonderful to see!

Materials: Washable paints in a variety of colors, paint brushes, large paper plate, large piece of heavy paper

Instruction:

- Do you know how relaxing it can be to mix paint? I had a friend who taught me that paint mixing can be more relaxing than even painting!

- Please choose as many paint colors as you like. You will be mixing paint colors to create a new color, so feel free to choose a few paints or many. It's up to you.

- Now that you have chosen your paints, squirt some of each color onto this paper plate.

- It's time to mix! Please use these paint brushes to pick up each color of paint you wish to use and place directly on this large piece of paper. Now, mix the paints with your brush, moving it in a circular motion.

- If you'd like, you can now move the paint brush in the opposite direction, while still moving it in a circular motion.

- Continue mixing as many different colors as you like, for as long as you need. There is no need to think about what you are doing, you are simply mixing paint colors to help you relax.

- Now that you are finished, tell me about this activity. How did it feel to mix colors? Did you notice any differences when mixing clockwise/counterclockwise? Was it easier or harder to just mix rather than actually paint a picture? Tell me more about that.

# No Talking Stick

Talking Sticks have been used often in counseling families and groups. The concept is that whoever is holding the talking stick is the talker, and the others are the listeners. Often, therapists will use an object such as a stuffed animal or a wand to act as a talking stick. I have found that many of my clients get "over-talked" to when they are feeling dysregulated and that words by others can cause even more trouble getting calm. Because of this, I invented the No Talking Stick, a simple tool that the child can hold to let others know, "I need a break!"

MATERIALS: A used paper towel roll, markers, various craft materials (sticky gems, feathers, stickers, etc.), glue/tape, and the "My No Talking Stick" poem are needed for this activity.

INSTRUCTIONS:

- Do you ever just need a break from others talking to you? Is it easier for you to calm down if you could just get a little bit of quiet? A lot of my clients have told me that when they are upset, the more others talk to them and the more they get angry!

- Sometimes we just wish we could say, "Stop talking," but we may think it's rude, be afraid we'll get in trouble, or it just doesn't come out right when we are angry. Don't you wish there was a way to let people know that we just needed a break for a bit to calm ourselves?

- Would you like to know a way to do just this? It's a craft I made up called a No Talking Stick. Using this paper towel roll, you can decorate it however you want with any of the supplies I have here. There is no wrong way to do this!

- When you are finished creating, we can roll up this poem and place it in your no talking stick, so others can know why we are using it. Of course, we will let your family members know, but the poem may help jog their memories, too!

My No Talking Stick

If you see me holding this no talking stick,
It means I need it calm,
To clear my head and think things through,
No need to be alarmed.

Please give me time to figure out
What I am feeling inside.
The quiet will help me think it through,
The stick will be my guide.

Worry Doll

Guatemalan worry dolls have been used for years as a visual way to place children's worries somewhere else outside of them. Tiny worry dolls and a container are used for children to verbalize their worry, holding the doll while they say it, then placing the doll in the container. In this activity, children make their own worry doll, which can be bigger in size and more tactile since chenille stems (pipe cleaners) are used. This activity can be difficult for tiny hands, or for children with fine motor difficulties, so therapists may need to provide some extra help.

MATERIALS: Chenille stems, many colors of embroidery floss, round wooden beads, permanent markers, scissors, and tape are needed for this activity.

INSTRUCTIONS:

- Have you heard of Guatemalan worry dolls? Children have used them for centuries to take their worries out of them! You see, children hold the worry doll, state what their worry is, and then "give" the worry to the doll. Don't worry, he/she can handle it!

- Today we are going to make a worry doll of our own! There are several steps to this activity, so we will both have to focus and concentrate *(lots of mindfulness!)*. I will be helping you every step of the way.

- *(See directions for making a worry doll on next page and follow slowly, step by step.)*

- We've done it! You now have your very own worry doll! Would you like to name him/her? How did it feel creating him/her? I noticed we were challenged several times, what made you not give up?

- What is the first worry you are going to give him/her? Let's give it to him/her now! Remember, he/she can handle it!

Worry Doll Directions

1. Take chenille stem of child's color choice and bend it in half.

2. Take some embroidery floss of child's color choice and wind it loosely around three fingers until child is happy with amount. (This will be the hair, so if children want longer hair they can wrap around more fingers, or around their entire hand. The key is to do this loosely.)

3. Carefully take the floss off of the child's hand, and place evenly into the crease of the chenille stem.

4. Have the client choose a wooden bead and draw a face on it using permanent markers.

5. Take the wooden bead (now a face) and place the two ends of the one chenille stem into the bead hole. (Make sure the hair is still in the crease of the stem!) Gently move the bead up the stem until it reaches the hair. (Now the bead is secure, and the hair is too!)

6. Take a second chenille stem and wrap around the center of the first stem to make arms. (The child may want to cut the stem to have shorter arms.)

7. Position the two ends of the first chenille stem to make them look like legs.

8. If clients want to, they can then use additional embroidery floss to wrap around parts of the body to make clothes. Some choose to do this, others do not. They may also choose to cut the hair at the loops, so it is straight.

9. Your worry doll is complete!

Worry doll named "Wanda" created by a nine-year-old client.

Three-Dimensional Interventions

Three-dimensional activities help clients focus on mindfulness, as well as creativity and mastery. The feelings children get from completing a somewhat challenging activity in a safe environment can do wonders for their self-concept. I've noticed that presenting attainable challenge activities in the playroom, and then having parents replicate these challenges at home, empowers my clients to be less hesitant towards trying something new in other settings.

Three-dimensional activities are impermanent in nature, which may create some difficulty with clients. 2-D pieces of art do not get taken apart, which allows children to take their masterpieces home. 3-D art is typically made from materials that either have to stay in the playroom or do not travel well. Therapists need to assess if they believe their clients are ready for the temporary nature of their artwork. This may seem silly, but I have had complete meltdowns in my office when children realized that it wasn't possible to take their block creation home! Of course, mild dysregulation is beneficial to process with the client by acknowledging their feelings and being with them through their expression, but take care to slowly introduce temporary masterpieces to clients who are intense in their dysregulation.

Balloon Squeeze Ball

Balloon squeeze balls are an excellent way for children to get any extra tension out of their hands. Squeezing seems to be relaxing for children and, often, additionally helps with focus and concentration. I have a sand tray in my office, so we all create the balloon squeeze balls with my sand. The children love being able to take some of my "magic sand" home! If you do not have a play therapy sand tray in your office, gallon bags with flour, rice, or pea beans work too. Sometimes my clients want to add beads or something harder into the balloon, which adds even more of a sensory experience!

MATERIALS: Two balloons, sand/flour/beans/rice, a funnel, shovel, and scissors are needed for this intervention.

INSTRUCTIONS:

- Sometimes when we are stressed we feel a lot of tension throughout our body. It can feel good to just SQUEEZE it out!

- Today we will make a balloon squeeze ball that you can put in your sensory bag and use whenever you need it. *(Sensory bag is an intervention in this book and is thoroughly explained.)*

- First you need to pick two balloons of any color. Please know that one balloon you will see when we are finished, and the other one you will not see. So, one balloon color doesn't really matter as much as the other balloon color.

- Great choosing your colors! Now, please let me know which balloon is the one we won't see. Okay, blow that one up and then hold it for about one minute. *(Younger clients may need help blowing the balloon. Also make sure they just hold it, not tie it.)*

- Alright, let all of the air out and dry the end where some spit may have settled.

- Now, one of us will be in charge of holding the funnel in the balloon, and the other one will be in charge of scooping the sand into the funnel, so it goes into the balloon. Which one would you like to do?

- Now that you have decided, let's get some magic sand into your balloon! We should try to fill the balloon all the way up. Because you blew up the balloon and held it for a minute, more sand will fit into it!

- Great job! Now, one of us needs to tie the balloon so the sand doesn't come out. *(It's always me ☺)*

- Next, please take your second balloon, blow it up, and hold for one minute, just like we did with the first balloon.

- Now please cut off the end of the balloon up about one inch. *(This makes it possible to wrap this balloon around the sand balloon.)* We will now wrap this balloon around the sand balloon. This is a VERY important step because the balloon could easily break if it didn't have this extra layer of protection!

- Great job! You now have your very own balloon squeeze ball! You can use it whenever you like and may keep it in your sensory bag.

Block Challenge

Challenge is an important part of the therapeutic relationship. Often, highly dysregulated children become frustrated very easily when they cannot do something right the first time and subsequently give up. Having these children experience a safe amount of challenge in the playroom can be the starting point for accepting challenges in other environments.

MATERIALS: Blocks of different shapes and colors are all that is needed for this intervention. If readers do not have blocks, simple colors and shapes can be designed on paper and cut out; then this could become a 2-D activity.

INSTRUCTIONS:

- Are you up for a challenge? Am I up for a challenge? Let's find out! Today we are going to challenge each other with blocks!

- I'm not sure how well I can do this, so let's start simpler and move our way up. Please take three blocks out of the bin. They can be any color or shape that you choose.

- Great! Now arrange these three blocks however you want on the floor. There is no wrong way to do this!

- Now that you are finished, I need to try to make the same design that you did. Wish me luck! *(I like to describe my process to myself but "out loud"—often known as the Whisper Technique, taught to me by Terry Kottman, creator of Adlerian Play Therapy.)*

- Okay, I think I got it! Let's both check my work.

- Now it's your turn. I'm going to make a three-block design and then you copy it. Wait until I'm finished just in case I decide to change it!

- I'm finished, so now you copy it. Let me know if you need any help.

- GREAT JOB, YOU DID IT! *(I then continue with four, five, etc. blocks, not stopping until I notice mild frustration at the level where we can work together to still complete.)*

- How did it feel when we did three blocks? I noticed you looked frustrated at six (or whatever number they get to) blocks, can you describe how that felt?

- Even though you were frustrated, you still worked it out. How did you do that?

- How does it feel to know you were frustrated, but you still completed it and did it correctly?

- Are there other times in your life when you feel frustrated— maybe at home or at school—when you may stop too soon? What did you do here when that happened that you can try during those times?

Marshmallow Creations

When I was a school counselor, my co-counselor did an activity in classroom guidance using marshmallows and toothpicks. It was a team building activity where groups of students would work together to make the tallest tower out of those items. I was surprised to see how focused the children were on this activity. There was something about using marshmallows, perhaps because they were playing with food, that seemed to make it less competitive and more fun!

I have modified this activity to allow for more of a non-directive approach. I don't give any structure as to what the clients should make; I allow for full creativity. This activity presents a nice amount of challenge in a safe and supportive environment. The children are very mindful while making these creations!

As an added bonus, quite often the first idea of the child changes and becomes something completely different. It is a great metaphor for how life changes can be unexpected yet okay.

MATERIALS: Mini marshmallows (about 50) and toothpicks (about 25) are needed for this intervention.

INSTRUCTIONS:

- Have you ever heard the expression, "Don't play with your food?" Well, today we are going to do just that!

- You'll notice I have a bag of marshmallows and toothpicks on the table. You are going to be able to create whatever you want using only these two items! The great thing about these two things is that they can be put together to make a 3-D creation if you choose, or you can keep your creation flat. There is no wrong way to do this!

- Feel free to start whenever you are ready, and you let me know when you are finished. I'll remain quiet so you can fully focus.

- Wow, you're finished! What a creation! Tell me about it. How did you decide what to create?

- Was this your first choice?

- Your second?

- If not your first choice, what made you change your mind?

- Did your senses notice anything while working with marshmallows and toothpicks? *(Usually they notice the smell and texture of the marshmallows.)*

- How was the extra sensory experience?

- Would you like to eat some of your creation?

- *(I make sure ahead of time that parents are okay with this, and we do set a limit on how many marshmallows can be eaten!)*

Clay Calm

Clay can be very soothing for many children. I have many different types of clay due to many of my clients having tactile sensory issues. It is a good idea to find a variety of clay textures, some being drier and less flexible, while others being wetter and more flexible. In my experience, my sensory avoiding tactile clients choose the dryer clay, whereas my sensory seeking ones choose the wetter clay.

MATERIALS: A small container of moldable, air-dried clay is needed for this activity.

INSTRUCTIONS:

- What does the word "calm" mean to you? Can you describe calm without using the word? It can be very hard describing feelings! It seems much easier to think of people, places, and things that help calm us, rather than come up with a definition of calm.

- I want you to think about people, places, and things that help you feel calm. Close your eyes if you wish, and I can guide you. Do you have a special calming person, someone who knows just what to say or do when you are upset? Do you have a special place you go when upset; a chill-out zone? Are there special things you can use to help you calm down and feel better?

- Please take some clay and create a sculpture of a person/place/ thing that helps calm you. You can choose whatever you wish, and there is no wrong way of doing this! Take your time on it, and let me know when you are finished. I will be quiet while you are creating so you can focus.

- Wow, you created your calm! Tell me about it. How did it feel creating it?

- Did you notice any new feelings arise while you created this?

- Which ones?

- What do you think you should do with the finished product?

- Can it be an additional thing to help you with calming?

Clay Calm named "Campfire" by a six-year-old client.
I allowed him to use two colors since this was important to him.
He chose to keep his creation as is so he could take it home.

Mindful Stone

Stones are wonderful tools to use as canvases for art activities. Children love the feel of stones, and they take their time picking out the one that is "just right" for their hands to hold. This activity could be completed with permanent markers as an alternative, but creating mindful stone collages are quite beautiful.

MATERIALS: A variety of stones, magazines, a sponge brush, and Mod Podge is needed for this activity.

INSTRUCTIONS:

- Today you will be able to create a very special stone. It will be your mindful stone that you can hold whenever you need some help feeling calm.

- Please pick your favorite stone. It may take some time to find your perfect mindful stone. Feel free to place several in your hand and hold them to see which one is best.

- Now that you have chosen your stone, let's look through these magazines. Remember, we are looking for pictures that look calming to you and that will fit on this stone.

- When you find the pictures you like, it's a good idea to tear them out instead of using scissors. The torn edges look really nice on the stone and fit well with collaging.

- Now, you can arrange the pictures however you like all over your stone. You may decide to put just one picture on your stone or overlap lots of pictures on your stone. Any way you choose is perfect! We will both try to remember how you want these pictures, for once we brush on the Mod Podge, we won't be able to move them!

- Now, take the sponge brush and dip it into the Mod Podge. Spread a layer of Mod Podge onto the rock, then place the pictures on top. Continue placing pictures until the rock is just how you like it. Then very carefully brush another layer of Mod Podge onto the rock and let's put it on the table to dry.

- *(This can take several hours to dry, so I suggest they keep the stone at the office where they can retrieve it at the next session. If they really want to take the stone home, I wait until the last five minutes, cover the stone with parchment paper, then put it in a gallon-sized plastic bag.)*

Mindful Stones we created at a children's
mindfulness retreat.

Mantra Stones

This intervention is similar to Mindful Stone except that the focus is on one word. Allowing children to pick their mantra word can help with calm focus during moments of dysregulation. I make sure I have smaller stones for this activity since we are only writing one word. Smaller stones are also more portable, so children can easily put these in their pockets and hold onto them wherever they go.

MATERIALS: A variety of stones and permanent markers or fine-line paint pens are needed for this intervention.

INSTRUCTIONS:

- Did you know that words are powerful? Words can uplift us, anger us, and more. Sometimes people say special words to themselves to help them cope with unpleasant feelings. A mantra word is one special word that you can use whenever you are feeling upset to remind you that you are strong and capable of working with your feelings.

- Please close your eyes and think about a time this week that was rough for you. What had happened? How were you feeling? Did you find anything that helped you cope? What did you need to feel better?

- Now let's think of one simple word. Is there a word that could have helped you remember how strong you were? There is no hurry thinking about this; it may take some time to come up with the "just right" word. *(I have magnetic adjectives of positive words on my file cabinet that we often use if the client is feeling stuck. These can be great tools to use!)* Let me know what word seems perfect for you.

- Now that you've picked your perfect word, please look at these stones placed here. Pick up as many as you like to test them out. Test them to see which one feels best in your hand and could fit your word. Let me know when you've found the best one.

- Now that you have your stone and your word, please take the markers of your choice and write your word on your stone. You can write the word big or small, one color or multicolor. You can even decorate with markers around your word if you so choose. There is no wrong way to do this!

- You have created your very own mantra stone! Carry it with you wherever you go and use it whenever you need some help with coping.

12

Movement Interventions

Moving is so important for both physical and mental health, and can be so beneficial in the therapy office! Studies have shown significant gains in attention and problem solving through movement; and since movement increases blood flow, it also provides more oxygen to the brain. When I was a teacher, I allowed students to move while they were memorizing important math concepts, and they all reported that this movement helped them focus and remember better.

Therapists with dedicated play therapy rooms often have movement take place organically during play. We have toys and objects that facilitate this, and movement is a big part of our sessions. Despite this, I still like to introduce mindful moving, which is slower in pace and involves thinking and concentration. This is especially useful to teach to my clients with ADHD—many of them exclaiming it's "impossible" or "uncomfortable" to move mindfully.

With practice, clients are able to successfully engage in mindful movements, and these movements help when difficult situations arise.

Slow it Down, Stan!

This may quite possibly be one of my favorite interventions that I use during my sessions. Witnessing the client go from a fast and furious mover to a mindful mover is quite amazing! This activity needs a lot of repetition and practice both in the therapy room and at home. I have even had school staff practice this intervention with all of the students after my child clients teach it to them!

A key to this game is to monitor your own movements, so sometimes you move faster than the child. Trust me when I say that if you don't, the child will always move faster than you! I want the children to feel successful and get an opportunity to say, "Slow it down, Stan!" to me. It's a fun way for them to monitor my movements as well as their own.

MATERIALS: Strips of paper listing common activities are needed for this intervention.

INSTRUCTIONS:

- Today we are going to try moving slowly. It's harder than it sounds! We are going to play a game called "Slow it Down, Stan."

- This basket is filled with folded-up strips of paper. Each paper strip has an activity on it that children may like to do. We will take turns picking a paper strip and reading what the activity is.

- Once we read the activity, we both will act out what the activity is. The trick is that we have to act it out moving as SLOWLY as possible! Let's see who can move slower. If I notice you may be moving faster than me, I may call out "Slow it down, Stan!" You may do the same to me!

- *(Assume child has just picked "throwing a football.")* Okay, you picked throwing a football. Let's both stand up facing each other so we can see how the other does. On the count of three, move your body as if you are throwing the football, but move as SLOWLY as you possibly can. One, two, three! *(Repeat this intervention four to six times until each person has chosen two or three activities to act out.)*

- Wow, we finished! What did you think? Was this game easy, difficult, or somewhere in between?

- How did it feel to slow your movements down? Describe that to me.

- Can you think of places where you may be getting into trouble or missing out on things because you are moving too quickly?

- Where are they?

- Do you think practicing "Slow It Down, Stan" may help?

- Why or why not?

Mirror, Mirror

I find this activity provides just the right amount of challenge for clients, as well as an exceptional way of working on mindfulness. The focus needed to follow my movements allows clients to actually "feel" mindfulness. I can purposely move slowly so my clients can experience what "slow" feels like in their bodies. It's important to remember that many of our clients are fast movers, so slow moving may be virtually unknown to them!

MATERIALS: Just your body!

INSTRUCTIONS:

- Today we are going to play a game called "Mirror, Mirror." You and I are going to take turns being the leader. If you are okay with it, I'll go first to show you how it's played.

- Let's sit down cross-legged and face each other. For starters, we are going to use just our hands. I'm going to hold both of my hands up, with my palms facing you. Now, you hold up your hands and place your palms close to mine, but not touching. Yes, just like that!

- I am now going to choose one of my hands to move. I'm going to move this hand very slowly in any way I choose. I could move it up or down, in circles or in a line. However my hand moves, you move your hand the same way. It may be kind of tricky at first, but I'll move very slowly so we both can do this together. Are you ready? I'll start.

- Great job! Now it's your turn. Choose one of your hands and move it very slowly however you would like. I'll try to follow your hand with my hand as closely as possible. If you're ready we can begin. *(Repeat with other hand; then the intervention can move to standing up and using head, arms, legs, feet, etc.)*

- What did you think of this activity? Was this easy or difficult? How were you able to follow my hand so well? While we were doing this did you notice anything else going on? *(Most of my clients say no, because they had to pay attention to how I was moving my hand.)*

- That focus is mindfulness! Mindfulness is when we just focus on what is going on right now, not on what happened at school or what will happen after you leave here. When we focus on the "right now," it can help us feel calmer and more focused.

- Practice this often with your family or friends. Not only will it help you feel calmer, but you will be helping them feel better too!

Act As If

When working with children in therapy sessions, it may become easy to only focus on the issues. Often enough we ask about what is wrong, how often they have been dysregulated, or what their anxiety or anger feels like. We may often ask about the symptoms of their diagnoses and the triggers they experience.

However, we tend to forget about focusing on wellness and all of the things that are positive and balanced in their lives. In this intervention, we discuss what it may look like to actually feel the opposite of what they are struggling with, and then we act it out. It is so much fun and can be practiced at home!

MATERIALS: No materials are needed for this activity.

INSTRUCTIONS:

- I bet you've had to talk a lot about what it feels like to be anxious. *(This can also be used for other emotions, but for clarity the focus is anxiety in this example.)* Some children have told me that speaking about their anxiety often causes even more anxiety!

- For one minute, let's just focus on one of the things that makes you anxious. What may that be? Walking into a room filled with people *(again, an example)* can cause anxiety! That is something we can definitely work on.

- Let's think about a person who seems to have no trouble walking into a room. Maybe it's someone you know or maybe it's a famous person. Who would you like to choose?

- Now tell me about this person and how they move into a room. Oh, I see *(and I start to act it out)* they hold their head up high, and they take long strides. They smile at the people in the room and then sit down at their seat. Well, this is fun to walk this way!

Would you like to try it? Walk with me, as if we have no anxiety at all! *(We do this for as long as they like.)*

- Now, I know it would probably be silly to walk into a room exactly like that, but can you maybe try one of the things we did next time you walk into a room?

- Maybe keep your head up?

- Maybe walk a little slower?

- Maybe say hi to one person?

- It may seem tricky at first, but I bet with practice you will be able to accomplish it!

Feelings Dance

Dancing can be fun and cathartic, and focusing on feelings while dancing can help illuminate even more how they feel in clients' bodies. I also find it informative to see movements my clients show that relate to their feelings. It helps me get a better view of my child clients outside of the therapy room.

MATERIALS: No materials are needed for this activity.

INSTRUCTIONS:

- Music can be an excellent coping skill to help us regulate our emotions. It can also feel so good to move our bodies to the music we enjoy!

- Today I get to learn more about you and what music you like. We can talk about different feelings you have felt lately and then choose moves that remind you of these feelings.

- Can you name a feeling that you have felt lately? *(Client names one.)* Let's think about that feeling. What does (happy, sad, mad, scared, etc.) feel like in your body?

- If that feeling had a body, how do you think it would move? Let's move our bodies how we think (happy, sad, mad, scared, etc.) would move. *(This activity can be repeated for a second, third, and fourth feeling.)*

- Did you notice any differences in how you moved depending on which feeling was moving? Tell me more about that. I wonder if we move differently when we feel different feelings. What do you think? Do you suppose that we could modify how we are feeling by moving in a different way? Maybe we can investigate that in the coming week and see!

Hand Jive

This activity is similar to Mirror, Mirror in that it follows the lead of the first person's hand movements. This activity has a different structure, however, where we take turns making up silly hand gestures, then we pick our top four for our personalized Hand Jive!

MATERIALS: No materials are needed for this activity.

INSTRUCTIONS:

- Our hands are amazing things! We can make up all kinds of gestures with our hands. Some gestures are friendly, such as waving or giving a thumbs up, while others aren't so friendly and can get us into trouble.

- Today we are going to take turns watching the other do some hand gestures. You can go first or I can. Whoever goes first can do a real or made up gesture with one or both hands. The follower will mimic this gesture as closely as possible. We don't have to get it right the first time; we can keep trying while having fun! Once we get the first gesture, we switch positions and the new leader gets to create a gesture. Any questions?

- *(After each of us has a turn creating three to four gestures.)* Wow, that was fun! What do you think about you and me creating our very own Hand Jive; a hand routine that is made special by you? Let's pick your favorite four gestures that we did and put them in an order that you like best.

- Now that you've picked your top four in the order you like best, let's practice! *(I also write it down so I don't forget; I have lots of Hand Jives to remember!)*

- What a great Hand Jive you have created! We can do this whenever you need to, maybe when you first come into a session! You can also teach it to your parents and friends, or even make up new ones for them! It takes focus and concentration to do, but boy is it fun!

Dice Moves

It requires a lot of mindfulness to focus on moving only parts of your body! The game Dice Moves practices just that! Depending on what is rolled, players may be moving one part of their body, one half of their body, or one side of their body. The primary motor cortex on the left side of the brain controls movement of the right side of the body and vice-versa. Practicing this can not only help with mindfulness, but also with cognitive flexibility.

MATERIALS: Dice and "Dice Moves!" sheet are needed for this activity.

INSTRUCTIONS:

- Today we are going to practice mindful moving. We will use a die and this sheet to see what we will need to move.

- Notice on this sheet that it states what/what side/what half of our bodies we need to move, but it does not say how. The roller gets to decide that! Maybe we flap, do circles, bend, shake—it's up to the roller!

- From this bag of colored dice, please choose whichever die you want. That is the one we will use for this game. You will also be able to take it home, along with the "Dice Moves!" sheet so you can also play with your family and friends.

- Whoever is the leader will get to roll the die five times. After each roll, we will take 20 seconds to complete the activity. The number on the die will decide what we move; the leader will decide how we move. We will repeat these four more times, then a new leader is chosen. If you're ready, let's begin!

- *(After playing the game two rounds, with each leader rolling five times.)* How did you feel in your body before/during/after playing? Were certain movements easier/more difficult than others? How so? Did you notice times where you had to focus more than at other times? Were you thinking about anything else when performing these moves? If not, then you experienced mindfulness!

Dice Moves!

Roll the die, see what number you get, then do the following for a count of 20:

Roll 1: Roller chooses any movement that only uses **hands**.

Roll 2: Roller chooses any movement that only uses **feet**.

Roll 3: Roller chooses any movement that only uses **upper half of body**.

Roll 4: Roller chooses any movement that only uses **lower half of body**.

Roll 5: Roller chooses any movement that only uses **left half of body**.

Roll 6: Roller chooses any movement that only uses **right half of body**.

All Terrain Walking

This activity allows children to move their body in various, fun ways while also using their imagination!

MATERIALS: Index cards with various surfaces written on them are needed for this activity. (Examples include mud, clouds, water, slippery rocks, trampoline, etc.)

INSTRUCTIONS:

- Do you think we may move our bodies differently depending on where we're walking? I know for me I move VERY differently on an icy driveway than on a driveway on a sunny and dry day!

- I have several index cards with different types of surfaces written on them. We can take turns picking one, and then acting out how we would move on these surfaces. If you're ready we can begin! *(I become very animated in this activity to help them feel more comfortable if there is any hesitation towards this activity.)*

- Now that was fun! What do you think about how we moved?

- How were our movements the same and how were they different?

- Did you have to pay more attention to some of your movements?

- Which ones?

- Can you think of times in real life when your movements may be different?

- How can practicing these help us be more mindful in our movements?

─ ⑬ ─
Games
Interventions

Simply put, games are fun! The joy both clients and therapists experience from participating together in a game is a sure-fire way to build rapport and trust in the therapeutic relationship. All too often, this generation of children is less likely to play games than in previous generations. Families are busier, neighborhoods may be less safe, and the electronics era has brought to us an entirely different type of "game." Typically, when I ask children if they'd like to play a game, they respond by stating that they don't see a video game console in my room! This is a reminder that we need to be ready to teach our clients games and not assume that they already know how to play them.

Many of us may have clients who become highly dysregulated when they lose a game. In these situations, I always start with a fun and completely non-competitive type of game. As they become successful at participating fully in these, I then introduce cooperative games. These games are set up in a way in which we both win or lose together. Cooperative games are wonderful ways to model appropriate winning and losing behavior! I rarely move on to one-on-one competitive games since I believe that my child clients experience these types of games enough in their daily life activities. I don't wish to be in competition with my clients. However, if clients want me to play a competitive game with them I agree, while processing through any dysregulation they experience while playing.

I included some of my clients' favorite games, but there are so many others to play. Use your imaginations, and also let your clients create games of their own. It is simply a wonderful way to fully play with your clients!

Where I Stand

This intervention allows clients to mindfully think about how they feel on various topics. The yarn shows a visible spectrum where clients can see that they may not have an opinion on one extreme or the other. This can be very helpful for our black and white, "all or nothing" thinkers who often are very rigid in their views. It's a good practice for them to begin seeing that there is often a middle ground for their thoughts and opinions.

MATERIALS: Yarn, two pieces of paper (one stating "always" and one stating "not at all"), and the Where I Stand sheet are needed for this activity.

INSTRUCTIONS:

- Notice that I have a long piece of yarn taped to the floor, along with two pieces of paper. On the left, the paper says, "Not at all," whereas on the right, "Always" is written.

- This will be a get-to-know-you activity where you will be able to move around a bit. You may find this easier than the classic worksheet-type questions that adults may ask.

- I'm going to read a statement from this sheet. I want you to think about how you feel about this statement. If you believe this statement is not at all like you, then you will move directly on top of the paper that says that. If you believe this statement is always like you, then you will stand on top of that piece of paper.

- Many of the questions may not have you feeling as strongly one way or the other. That is what the yarn is for. You may move and stand anywhere on the yarn to show how you feel about the statement. The closer you are to each side of paper shows me whether you feel more or less with each statement.

- There is no wrong way to do this; you simply move wherever you feel you should stand after each statement. If you're ready we can begin.

- Now that we've played the game, what did you learn about yourself?

- Were you surprised by where you stood on some of the questions?

- How so?

- Were any of the questions difficult to answer?

- Which ones?

- Tell me about the times you were having difficulty deciding where to stand. How can we think about this in real life when we have to make decisions on how we feel?

- Can we always be "all yes" or "all no" about something?

Not at all   Always

Where I Stand

- I am a happy person

- I like to have people around me

- I sleep well at night

- I eat healthy

- I have friends who care for me

- My teacher likes me

- My parents love me

- I help my siblings

- I do well in school

- I am honest

- I have meltdowns

- I do my homework

- I play computer games

- I hit when I'm angry

- I am smart

Cotton Ball Target

Working on slow, mindful breathing with clients can be a challenge. The breathing interventions explained in this book are very helpful tools for this. Games can also be a fun way to introduce mindful breathing, while also working on healthy challenge and having fun! This is a simple game that can be played in a variety of ways, and the rules can be made up as the game is being played. My clients often choose to play this game, and the materials are so simple that this can also be played at home.

MATERIALS: Cotton balls, straws, and a paper circle are needed for this activity.

INSTRUCTIONS:

- I have quite the challenge for us today! We are going to try to get cotton balls on this circle by blowing through a straw. Sounds easy, right? Not so much! We will take turns being the leader, and the leader gets to decide where the circle is placed and how many blows will be allowed to try to get the cotton ball on the target. It's definitely a challenge, but a fun one!

- I will start since I've played this game before. I'm going to set the target on this table. We both can sit on chairs. Our cotton balls can be placed right on the edge of the table. I say our challenge is to get the cotton ball to the target in three blows. If we don't get it the first time, we can keep trying until we get the cotton ball on the target. Ready to try it? Let's go! *(Begin to play.)*

- Well, it took us several tries, but we did it! What did you notice about your blowing? *(Typically, my clients blow way too hard initially and learn they have to slow down and blow more softly.)* Yes, you had to control your blowing a bit, didn't you? Otherwise the cotton ball would fly right off of the table! How did it feel to blow slower?

(Typical responses are "calmer," "more controlled," "quieter," etc.) It's interesting how we can control our blowing to master this game!

- Now, it's your turn! Place the circle wherever you like. Now, place the cotton balls wherever you want them to be. How many blows should it take to get to the target? Before we start, how do you think we should blow?

- We can continue playing this game however long you like, with each of us taking turns being the leader. You can also take this home and practice with your entire family. Notice how you feel in your body after playing this game. You may be feeling differently after not only mastering this activity, but also controlling your blowing!

Sticker Hide and Seek

Hide and Seek is a classic children's game that everyone seems to know how to play. I'm often asked by children if we can play it, but I really don't have the office space to do so. I devised this alternative in an effort for my children to still be able to have fun seeking something while also using mindfulness and focus when looking. The stickers they find still have a paper backing so they can decide if they want to put the stickers on themselves, collect them to take home, or create a sticker work of art when finished.

MATERIALS: A variety of large stickers with paper backings are needed for this intervention; plastic bags, art paper, and markers may also be useful if the clients want to take the stickers home or create a picture from them.

INSTRUCTIONS:

- Have you ever played Hide and Seek? It's fun to look for people, isn't it? You have to really concentrate, and not only look, but also listen for the person to find them!

- My room is too small to play Hide and Seek the traditional way, so I invented a new way to play it. In here we play Sticker Hide and Seek! All of these stickers in this tub may be used. The hider will take five stickers and hide them anywhere in this room. When hiding, **don't take the paper backing off, that will be for later.** The seeker will close his/her eyes and wait until the hider says it is time. The seeker will then look for the stickers and has three choices once he/she finds them. He/She may:

  - Stick the sticker on his/her clothes/hands/face

  - Collect them in a plastic bag

  - Place them on the craft table to make a picture out of them

- Are you ready to play? Would you like to be the hider or the seeker? Okay, now that we have decided, let's play!

- *(We take turns hiding and seeking. When I am the seeker I put the stickers on me to make the game even sillier, but they can choose any of the three options.)*

- We finished the game. Look at how many stickers you found! Was it easier or more difficult to play Hide and Seek this way?

- Tell me how you were able to find the stickers so well?

- Did you notice you had to focus extra hard?

- Were you thinking about anything else while looking or were you just thinking about where the stickers were?

- If you were just thinking about the sticker, THAT is mindfulness!

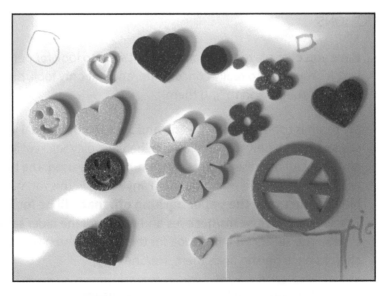

"My Family Sticker Picture" created by a
5-year-old client after playing Sticker Hide and Seek.

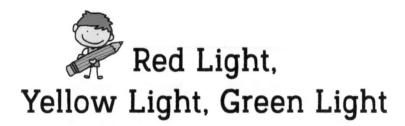

Red Light, Yellow Light, Green Light

This is a variation of the classic Red Light, Green Light game, where players would run whenever the leader yelled "Green Light!" then stop when the leader yelled "Red Light!" If you have ever tried playing this with clients who dysregulate easily, you may understand why the yellow light needed to be added! It's important for me to teach my clients that we often have a "yellow zone" that occurs between feeling good and feeling explosive. By practicing this game, my clients begin to see how a middle ground is present.

MATERIALS: Nothing is needed for this activity.

INSTRUCTIONS:

- Have you ever played Red Light, Green Light? It's a fun game where the leader yells "Green light," and the players run, then "Red light," and the players stop. It can be TOUGH to go from running to stopping!

- I made up a game called Red Light, Yellow Light, and Green Light. It's just as fun as the original but played a bit differently. First of all, instead of running forward, we just move our bodies however we want, since there isn't enough room in our space to run. Second of all, I added in a yellow light, which means we SLOW DOWN in our moving, but don't completely stop.

- So, you can be the leader first or I can. When the leader yells "Green light," we will move our bodies as fast as we can! When the leader yells "Yellow light," we will move our bodies SLOWLY. When the leader yells "Red light," we will completely stop our bodies. The leader can choose to yell whatever color he/she wishes.

- If you're ready, let's begin! *(We play the game.)*

- Now that we are finished, how did you like the game?

- If you have played the original before, how was this different?

- Was it easier or more difficult to have the yellow light added?

- Is it easy or difficult to move your body quickly/slowly/not at all?

- Are there times at home or school when it's important to do red/yellow/green light movements? Tell me about that.

Pebble Feelings

There are two variations on how I play this game with my clients. Due to this, I will simply explain how to complete each intervention without using the dialogue format.

MATERIALS: Small pea pebbles, seven paper plates (one for happy, sad, mad, scared, excited, and two blank), and a marker are needed for this intervention.

INSTRUCTIONS:

Variation One

In this variation, I allow the clients to add two additional feelings to our game and write each of them on a paper plate. I then give them the bag of pea pebbles and explain how we not only have different feelings throughout our day, but different intensities of feelings. I ask them to look at each plate with the feeling word, then take their pebbles and decide how much they have been feeling each one. They determine how much by the number of pea pebbles they place on each plate. I give them time to do this activity, since they often go back and change the number in each plate. I have found clients are very mindful when completing this activity! We then process how much they have been experiencing each feeling and what led them to put those amounts with each feeling.

Variation Two

In this variation, I have the clients add two additional feelings to our game and write each of them on a paper plate. Then, we line the paper plates up however the clients chooses, and we choose a place to sit about five feet away from the plates. Next, we take turns tossing five pebbles at a time and see where they land. If they land on a feeling plate, the thrower shares what has happened lately that created that particular feeling. If it lands in between two plates, the thrower explains a situation that could cause those two feelings. If the five feet distance seems too easy, we will scoot back a foot to make this game more of a challenge. We play until each of us has been able to express at least four situations.

Therapy Ball Fun

There have been many interventions created using balls with various tasks on them. Most play therapy stores will have a variety of therapy balls you can choose from, focusing on topics ranging from anger to social skills. I like to create my own therapy balls using small beach balls that can be purchased in bulk from party supply websites. They are an inexpensive way to create a therapy ball specific to the client. The therapy balls can also be taken home so the clients and their families can practice daily.

MATERIALS: A small beach ball and a permanent marker are needed for this activity.

INSTRUCTIONS:

(There are many ways you can create your own therapy ball! For this example, we are creating a coping skills therapy ball.)

- It can be really difficult to remember how to calm down when we are upset! We've practiced calming down when we are at a "3" because we know that is the perfect time to calm since we are still in control *(see Pre-Intervention: The Thermometer in this book).*

- Sometimes if we make a game out of calming down it really helps us laugh and forget all about being upset! Having fun is such a wonderful tool for regulating!

- Today we will create your very own therapy ball. You can pick from any of these beach balls to use.

- Now, you or I can blow up the beach ball. Once we have blown it all the way up, we need to put the plug in so the air doesn't come out.

-

- Let's think about the last time you were upset. If that's too hard, we can think about any time that you have been upset or your upset triggers. Take a few minutes to think about your triggers, and then we can talk about them.

- Now that we've discussed your triggers, do you remember what you were able to do—either alone or with help—to calm down? When we think of something, you or I can write it on one color of the therapy ball *(all of the beach balls I have are striped with six colors)*.

- Wow! We've written on the therapy ball cookie breathing, clay squeezing, time out in canopy, push-ups, smelling peppermint oil, and eating a snack. Great job!

- Now, let's play! We can toss the ball to each other, and while it's in the air, the thrower can call out "thumb," "pointer," "middle," "ring," or "pinky!" When the catcher has the ball, he/she needs to do whatever coping skill is being touched with that particular finger. If we catch the ball with both of our hands, we can pick from either hand.

- Now that we are finished, what did you think about this activity?

- Did you enjoy being surprised at what coping skill you had to do?

- Was turning coping skill practice into a game fun for you?

- Where else can you practice this?

Storytelling Interventions

For centuries, storytelling has been used to build a sense of community among cultures. It is amazing to think about how many stories have been passed down from generations ago! From fairy tales to Greek and Roman myths, storytelling can be an important tool towards creating bonds with clients.

Storytelling also provides important metaphors that can directly align with the experiences of our clients. When we create stories using animals or other characters, it creates a safe distance from the clients while also providing therapeutic tools to help with issues they encounter. When clients create stories, it gives therapists a glimpse into their inner worlds and the gifts and challenges they possess within them.

The storytelling techniques I detail in this book provide a fun way to introduce clients to the art of creating both oral and written stories. As clients become more adept at this process, they can begin to create even more stories, often without having any directions given to them before starting. When working with children, many of them are uninterested in writing, perhaps because of the amount of writing they are expected to do at school, so be ready to either be their scribe or stay true to the oral tradition of storytelling where no writing occurs.

Comic Strip Mindful Story

Social stories are used often with children on the autism spectrum when learning something new. I have found the Comic Strip Template I created to be a useful tool in helping children think about how they can help themselves calm when feeling dysregulated. For my clients who do not like to draw, I always have magazines on hand that they can cut out characters and glue onto the sheet, as well as a variety of stickers. Clip art online can also be very handy if you have easy access to a printer.

MATERIALS: Colored pencils or markers, magazines, stickers, and a Comic Strip Template are needed for this activity.

INSTRUCTIONS:

- It is so important to take care of ourselves and to give our brains and bodies small breaks when needed!

- Sometimes it is hard to remember we need breaks until we get to the point where we're so upset that we're out of control! It is so much nicer to really notice when we are starting to get upset and take care of ourselves at that moment.

- You may notice on the table I have a Comic Strip Template. Some of the boxes already have words to help us get started, and some of the boxes are blank. Let's read the boxes with words together and then decide how to fill in each empty box.

- Now that we've completed the words to the comic strip, let's think about illustrating it! Would you like to use markers to draw yourself, or look through magazines? We can even look up clip art on the computer if you have a specific idea of what you want as an illustration! I also have stickers to decorate your comic strip.

- Fill in your comic with illustrations of your choice; there is no wrong way to do this! When you are finished, we can read the comic strip again and look at the pictures you created as well!

- Now that we are done, what do you think of your very own comic strip? Could it be useful to you? When? Where do you think you can place this comic strip to help you remember to calm?

My Mindful Comic Strip

Being mindful can be tough...

I can

I can

I know how to be mindful!

Sentence Story

Silly sentence stories can be mindful when the focus is on what's in front of you!

MATERIALS: No materials are needed for this activity, but paper and a pencil can be used for this activity if the client wants the therapist to be a scribe.

INSTRUCTIONS:

- Today we are going to work on being mindful in a fun and silly way. You and I are going to make up a silly story together!

- We will each take turns making up one sentence/line of our story. We are not going to write this story down, unless you really want to, in which case I'll be the scribe. We can make up any sentence we want, except for one rule: **Something we see, hear, smell, touch, or taste in the playroom has to be in each sentence!**

- We will really have to focus on where we are to create this story, won't we? Remember that this story should be silly and fun! There is no wrong way to make up this story!

- Whoever starts may say "Once upon a time" and then complete the sentence/line. Then the second person adds a sentence— don't forget to add a sight/sound/smell/taste/touch from the playroom. A good story should have at least 10 sentences, so once we have 10 sentences either of us can choose to say, "The End" whenever we feel it sounds right.

- Are you ready? Let's begin!

- Now that we are finished with our story, what should the title be? What kind of story would you call it? How were you able to focus so well on the senses in the playroom? Was it easier or harder to have to take turns?

The following is a Sentence Story completed with a 10-year-old client on the autism spectrum. The title was picked after processing. The client's responses are in bold italics.

He wanted me to be the scribe.

The Silly Train

Once upon a time there lived a giant shark named Thomas. ***Thomas really wanted to be a train not a shark.*** "Oh, how I wish I could be a train!" Thomas said as a car whooshed by. ***If I was a train I could smell peppermint whenever I went to the North Pole to meet Santa!*** Meeting Santa would be wonderful for Thomas; he imagined the snow would feel like touching sand. ***Thomas ate some fruit snacks because he liked them.***

While he ate the snacks, he decided he would be silly and act like a train! *(The client turned on my sound machine to train.)* "***Wwwhhhhhooooooo! All aboard,"*** **Thomas said!** Suddenly Thomas realized that he was moving as fast as a train and was going straight on the play streets to the North Pole! ***He was going to meet Santa Claus! He was going to make Santa make him be a train!*** *(The client went twice because he was excited, and I had no problem with this.)* He heard cars and trucks and birds and talking all of the way to the North Pole. ***He saw Santa and said, "Santa make me a train," and Santa said, "Ho ho, ok," and he did!***

From that day on Thomas was happy and smiled really big, and he lived happily ever after. ***The end!***

My Melody

This intervention is very popular with clients of all ages, including adults. The free *Relax Melodies* app has the different sounds build on each other, allowing clients to create their very own melodies. This app also enables each chosen sound to have volume control, giving clients even more choice on how their melody sounds.

I write the melodies they choose onto an index card and place this is their sensory bags (page 154). Both parents and teachers tend to have tablets available with headphones so children can listen to their melody if feeling dysregulated.

MATERIALS: A smart phone/tablet with music app (my personal favorite is the free app on Apple and Android called Relax Melodies), an index card, and a pencil is needed for this intervention.

INSTRUCTIONS:

(Directions are explained as if we are completing the Sensory Bag intervention and are at the part where we focus on our ears.)

- Now, let's think about our ears. Yes, our poor ears! Sometimes they have to hear so many loud and unpleasant noises that they just need a break!

- Did you know that you can calm yourself down by taking an ear break? Well, it can be a bit trickier, but you can! We have to make sure when we take ear breaks that we aren't disrupting people around us. Since you may be taking your sensory bag to school, we will focus on an ear break that I know your teacher has.

- We will use my tablet to use the app called *Relax Melodies*. Do you see all of the brown squares with objects on them? Each of those squares is a sound. Press some now if you would like to hear them.

(Once they do this, they notice that when a second sound is pressed, the first sound can still be heard. They are typically surprised since most apps will stop the first sound and then only play the second.)

- Wow, did you notice that we can hear both sounds? If you press a third or a fourth sound we will then hear four sounds! Pretty amazing, isn't it? That is how you can make your very own relax melody!

- I would like for you to take your time and pick the perfect amount of sounds for you that will become your relax melody. Notice that each sound has a volume control, so some of your objects can be louder or softer than the others.

- Take your time with this, and let me know when you are finished. I will then write down your relax melody on this index card so you will know exactly what it is.

- Now that you are finished what did you think about this activity?

- Did you find it relaxing listening to the different sounds?

- Could you give your melody a title?

- Would you like to create a second melody?

- Are there any other places besides school where you could listen to this?

Dice Roll Story

This intervention is similar to the Sentence Story but with some changes. We do some pre-planning before, and then we take turns creating the story.

MATERIALS: Two dice and the "Dice Roll Planning Sheet" are needed for this intervention. If the client wants the story scribed, paper and pen should be available.

INSTRUCTIONS:

- Working together to make up a story can be a fun activity! When people are telling a story, they are being very mindful and focusing on how to best make the story flow. It can be more of a challenge working in pairs to create a story, but it also allows us to see that not fully knowing how something is going to go can be okay!

- For this activity, let's first look at our Planning Sheet. Notice the planning sheet has boxes for People, Places, Things, and Feelings. You and I will take turns rolling a die for each box. You can roll for two of the boxes, and I can roll for the other two. Whatever number we get, that is how many people/places/things/feelings we need in the story! We can use tally marks on this sheet so we can easily cross the items off once we say them.

- Let's roll and see how many people/places/things/feelings we need in our story!

- Now that we've completed that, it's time to create our story! We can just say it out loud, or I can scribe it for us so you have a copy to take home. We can each say up to two sentences before the next person gets a turn.

- Don't forget how many people/places/things/feelings we need in our story! When we say one, let's remember to cross it off so we can keep track. When we have completed all of them, we can decide together when to end the story. Ready?

- *(Once the story is completed.)* What a story we just created! How did you like completing this activity?

- How was it rolling for the numbers?

- Any feelings come up with that?

- Did you find it easy or difficult to create this story with me?

- Was it easy or difficult to have a certain number of people/places/things/feelings in the story?

- Tell me more about this experience. Should we give our story a name?

- If so, what would be a good one?

Dice Roll Planning Sheet

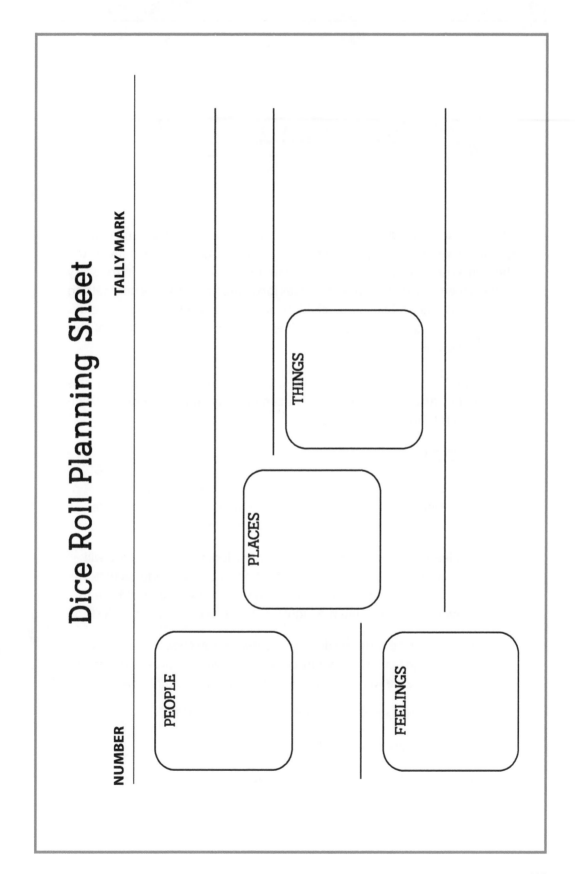

NUMBER

TALLY MARK

PEOPLE

PLACES

THINGS

FEELINGS

Story Picture Walk

This is a well-known strategy used by early childhood educators and reading specialists when helping children learn to read. Instructors will invite the children to go on a picture walk to help them find valuable clues in the story to assist them with the sight words. I was fortunate to work in a school setting where I was able to hear some children worry less about the context clues and let their imaginations go wild! These children are the authors of this therapeutic intervention!

MATERIALS: Various picture books without words are needed for this intervention. As a substitute, therapists can make picture books of their own using clip art from their computers.

INSTRUCTIONS:

- Look at these books I have placed here. These are picture books, meaning they have no words. Children and adults can enjoy these books since they get to use their imaginations in any way they choose.

- Please choose whichever picture book looks nice to you. We will make up our own story using this book! For each page/picture, we will make up a sentence to go with that picture. We don't have to worry about picking the "right" sentence because this is OUR story!

- We can take turns making up a sentence. You choose if you would like to go first, or if I should. Don't forget, we can make up whatever sentence we want! *(We now complete the story picture walk.)*

- Wow, what a story! How did you like creating this?

- Was it easier or more difficult to not have words?

- Did you like sharing the story or would you have rather made the entire story up on your own?

- How fun it is to use our imaginations to become authors!

15

Puppet Interventions

Puppets are a staple item in a play therapy room! They have been used for years by Play Therapists and are some of the first items we purchase. I'll never forget my first puppet, a small hedgehog, which I still have. I was a school counselor at the time and would do classroom guidance lessons in grades kindergarten through third. Having been a former high school teacher, I found the activity level and exuberance of these young children quite foreign! I was struggling to find a way to connect with these children in a meaningful way–to create a calmer space so they could really benefit from the guidance lesson. On a whim, I decided to bring my hedgehog puppet to the classrooms. This puppet has small legs that can easily hide his face, wave, or rub his belly. Whenever the children were becoming too dysregulated, Harry (the hedgehog's name) would quickly cover his eyes and I would quietly say, "Oh no! Harry is afraid by all of the noise!" The children would instantly quiet and be so happy when Harry's hands would move and he would be present with them again!

I am aware that many of you may not have the resources, space, or funds to have a variety of puppets in your playroom. For this reason, I included interventions on how to create both sock and finger puppets. These are fun to make and allow the children to take home to have fun with their families. One bag of socks can create twelve sock puppets and one pair of white gloves can make ten finger puppets! This is surely a cost-effective way to have puppet play in your office.

If you are looking to purchase puppets, it is always good practice to have the following types to allow for specific play themes to emerge:

- **Nurturing puppets** (rabbits, elephants, etc.): To allow for the play theme of nurturing and caring for others

- **Aggressive puppets** (bears, alligators, etc.): To allow for aggressive play themes

- **Fantasy puppets** (dragons, wizards, etc.): To allow for fantasy and imaginative play

- **People puppets of various skin tones**: To allow for metaphor play specific to families. Clients will often use animals to do this too, but having people puppets can be a nice addition. I also have a puppet police officer, doctor, and fire fighter, which has proven beneficial to children who have had trauma the incidents occur.

Make a Finger Puppet

I used to buy finger puppets for puppet play until I learned how to make my own. Children love to make these puppets and to be able to bring them home. Given the small number of fabric gloves I keep in my play therapy room, I limit each client to making two finger puppets per session. One pair of fabric gloves makes 10 puppets, so not many gloves are needed!

MATERIALS: Fabric gloves (found at most garden stores), felt/fabric, embroidery floss, googly eyes, permanent markers, sequins, scissors, and glue are needed for this intervention.

INSTRUCTIONS:

- Using scissors, cut one of the fingers off of the fabric glove.

- Glue around the seam where you just cut and press lightly. (This can be skipped, but the finger puppet may fray with continued use.)

- Take a piece of felt or fabric, cut to preferred size, then glue around the edge of the finger. (The felt/fabric will be the body of the puppet and additionally hides the children's hands.)

- Glue googly eyes onto the finger.

- Draw a nose and mouth with permanent markers.

- Cut embroidery floss and glue onto puppet for hair.

- Decorate the felt/fabric with sequins.

- You have a finger puppet!

Make a Sock Puppet

I have a large assortment of beautiful puppets in my therapeutic playroom, but I always want an alternative toy that children can make and take home. Initially, we would create puppets out of paper bags, but many of the children did not seem to like these as much as fabric-styled ones. I then learned how to make an easy sock puppet, and these have been a hit!

I make sure to buy very soft, plain white men's crew socks, so they fit longer on children's hands and aren't too tight. One six-pack of socks makes 12 puppets, so this is an inexpensive item to make. I limit the children to one sock puppet created per session since they do take a bit of time and I want to make sure we have time to create a puppet show. We always have my puppets to fall back on for multiple characters!

MATERIALS: One white sock, permanent markers, googly eyes, buttons, pom poms, construction paper, yarn, scissors, and fabric glue are needed for this activity.

INSTRUCTIONS:

- Place the sock onto the child's hand, making sure the heel of the sock is by the palm.

- Have the child place his/her thumb in the heel of the sock, then have his/her move the thumb and fingers together to begin making the puppet's mouth shape.

- While the puppet is on the child, make two small dots about one inch above the seam for eyes. Place one dot below and between the two dots for the nose.

- Have the child take off the sock and lay flat on the table. He/she may now choose to use googly eyes, buttons, and/or pom poms for the eyes and nose.

Place one drop of fabric glue onto the eye and nose dots, then place the chosen items for the eyes and nose on top of the glue.

- Hair can be made by cutting pieces of yarn and gluing on the top of the sock.

- A mouth can be colored in with permanent markers.

- The child can decorate the body of the sock however he/she wants.

- The child now has a sock puppet!

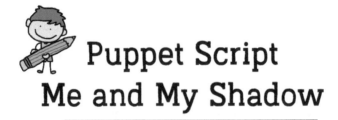

Puppet Script
Me and My Shadow

There are so many wonderful ways to play with puppets, and therapists are excellent at creating puppet scripts. Children also come up with imaginative scripts and often like to create as we are playing! I wanted to include two puppet scripts I use often, especially with more concrete thinking children who do not feel entirely comfortable with using their imaginations or feeling put "on the spot" to create a script. This particular script works well for working through alternatives to problematic behaviors.

MATERIALS: One puppet can be used for this script. The puppet can be one that the client made or one from the therapist's collection.

INSTRUCTIONS:

Step 1: Clients share an example of something that happened in which they did not respond in a healthy way.

Step 2: Clients choose which puppet they will be using for the puppet show (only one is needed).

Step 3: Clients learn that the puppet is their "shadow," which, in this show, is the healthy and calm figure that helps make good decisions.

Step 4: Clients decide if therapist will be the shadow or if they would like to be the shadow as well as themselves. (Typically, I ask to be the shadow for the first few times this intervention is being completed to make sure positive coping skills are suggested.) The therapist is also available to be other characters who may be involved in the situation.

Me and My Shadow Script

Scene 1: What is the problem? What happened? Who was part of the problem? When and where did this happen? Act this out!

Scene 2: The shadow steps in. He/she explains what the lead character can do to stay healthy and safe. The shadow helps the lead character calm down. Act this out!

Scene 3: The lead character follows the shadow's advice. The lead character does not get into trouble because he/she made the healthy choice! Act this out!

Puppet Script
My Shadow and Me

This script is very similar to Me and My Shadow, only this time the clients are the wellness gurus! I typically do the first puppet script for several sessions to introduce the idea of choosing safe and healthy behaviors. I do this because quite often they need me to be the shadow and give alternatives to problematic behaviors. Once they seem to have built up a healthy coping skills repertoire, I introduce this script, where the puppet is the one who really needs the help!

MATERIALS: One puppet can be used for this script. The puppet can be one that the client made or one from the therapist's collection.

INSTRUCTIONS:

Step 1:   The therapist shares an example of something that can happen to children in which they do not respond in a healthy way.

Step 2:   Clients choose which puppet they will be using for the puppet show (only one is needed).

Step 3:   Clients learn that **they** are their puppet's "shadow," which, in this show, is the healthy and calm figure that helps make good decisions.

Step 4:   Clients and therapist decide if any other characters are needed for this situation. (Typically, I pick a situation where there may be only one other character that I can easily play. I really want the client to focus on healthy coping skill suggestions!)

My Shadow and Me Script

Scene 1: What is the problem? What happened? Who was part of the problem? When and where did this happen? Act this out!

Scene 2: The shadow (now the client!) steps in. He/she explains what the lead character (now the puppet) can do to stay healthy and safe. The shadow helps the lead character calm down. Act this out!

Scene 3: The lead character follows the shadow's advice. The lead character does not get into trouble because he/she made the healthy choice! Act this out!

— (16) —
Sensory Interventions

I have been fortunate to meet and learn from many occupational therapists while working with clients on the autism spectrum. They have taught me the great value of sensory regulation within my clients (and myself)! It is so important for all children, but especially those with ASD, ADHD, and anxiety, to have a calm and pleasant sensory environment, as well as sensory interventions for when dysregulation occurs. Working with clients, parents, and teachers on creating these environments has been invaluable to my practice!

I first introduce readers to the Sensory Bag intervention. I complete this intervention with every single client. I make the assumption that all of my clients become dysregulated—just like every person on the planet! Whereas neurotypical children and adults can often calm themselves somewhat easily, our ASD, ADHD, and anxiety-diagnosed clients find this extremely difficult. Creating the sensory bag and working through various sensory interventions have been the game changers in my clients' road to healing.

I highly recommend all therapists research the sensory needs of children and begin incorporating a sensory-friendly therapy space as soon as possible!

Sensory Bag

Creating sensory bags is something I do early in the sessions, and often. They are a wonderful tool to help my clients regulate in any setting! These have been so successful that parents often replicate them and have multiple sensory bags at home, in the car, at school, etc. Schools have been very receptive to them as well and have added this intervention in my clients' IEPs and 504 plans. I have had several teachers who were so impressed with the effectiveness of the sensory bags that they made it an intervention for all of their students!

Using a ticket system, the child could hand the teacher a ticket then go to the "sensory station," grab his/her sensory bag, and take some time regulating. I love when I hear teachers doing this, for it not only normalizes the need to regulate for my clients, but also can help clients who are often quiet about their dysregulation find a way to cope!

In my office, I have a six-drawer rolling cart for all of my sensory bag items. This allows easy access for when a sensory bag is first created, as well as future access when refills are needed. My clients bring their sensory bags in often, needing to refill any items that have been used throughout the week. I do highly recommend only having one sensory item for each sense so the bag remains uncluttered and easy to access. I've seen many clients stuff so much into their bags that they can't find what they need!

MATERIALS: Many materials are needed for this intervention, so I will first explain the sensory bin setup and materials needed, and then explain the interventions.

INSTRUCTIONS:

1. Sensory Bin Setup:

I have each of the senses in a six-drawer rolling cart. You can modify however is needed.

- **Drawer 1: Eye Break Items:** Travel magazines, several large rocks, paint pens, mini mandala coloring book, several eight-pack crayons

- **Drawer 2: Nose Break Items:** Essential oils (all are researched to make sure they are safe for children), cotton balls, elastic cord, lava beads

- **Drawer 3: Hand Break Items:** Balloons, funnel, bags of sand/flour/rice, mini containers of play clay

- **Drawer 4: Mouth Break Items:** A variety of non-perishable foods that can either be chewed or sucked on; my drawer typically has organic fruit snack packets and hard candies (good because, although they are candy, they are extremely difficult to chew on so children slowly suck on them and one is typically all that is needed)

- **Drawer 5: Ear and Body Break Items:** Index cards, permanent marker, bag of dice, table template with six rows and five columns

- **Drawer 6: Bag Storage:** Gallon bags, snack bags

2. Sensory Interventions:

Eye Break: Choose from:

- Jump in the Picture (page 157)

- 10-minute mandala coloring (make sure you have mini mandalas that are simple and easy to color in under 10 minutes)

- Mindful Stone (page 100)

Nose Break: Choose from:

- Lava Bead Bracelet (page 164)

- Cotton Ball Scent (page 168)

Hand Break: Choose from:

- Balloon Squeeze Ball (page 92)

- Clay Calm (page 98)

Mouth Break: Choose from:

- Chew Time: Take three packages of organic fruit snacks (discuss only eating one at a time and have parent have extras on hand if oral approaches are often used by the child)

- Suck Time: Take three pieces of hard candy (again, discuss sucking one at a time and one per sensory break, and have parents have extra)

Ear Break: One choice *(ear is more difficult since it's important not to disrupt others while regulating)*

- My Melody (page 137)

Movement Break: One choice *(often this is saved to be completed with an entire family or classroom as a prevention activity)*

- Dice Moves (page 114)

3. How to Conduct the Sensory Bag Creation Session

I simply inform the client that we are going to make a sensory bag for them to take with them whenever they need to take a break. They get very excited when I roll the cart over to them! We then go through each sense, and I explain the choices. They choose which they want to do, and we complete the activity and then put it in their bag. When completed, I write each intervention on an index card, and then bring the parent in to explain the bag. I instruct the parents to initially help their child remember about the sensory bag whenever they first notice the child is dysregulating. This can easily be done by stating in a sing-song voice:

"Oh, I believe you may be getting dysregulated. Do you need an eye break? An ear break? A nose break? A mouth break? A hand break? A body break?"

Presenting it in this fashion minimizes any resistance the child may feel from needing a break. Often times my parents will tell me their child simply won't do an intervention. When I ask how they present it, it often sounds punitive when the parents suggest it to the child. It's important to be calm, pleasant, and mindful when presenting interventions to children!

This intervention takes the entire session, sometimes two if the client is very thoughtful during intervention completion.

Be prepared to only have this activity scheduled for the session.

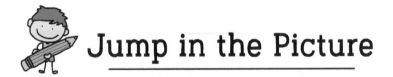

Jump in the Picture

This is one of my most requested interventions! When I conduct trainings nationwide, I often include this intervention for participants to try. Adults love it too and are surprised by how relaxed and happy they feel after completing it!

MATERIALS: A variety of travel and family magazines are needed for this intervention.

INSTRUCTIONS:

- Did you know that we have very powerful brains? Well, we do! Our brains are so powerful that just thinking about smelling chocolate chip cookies can have our brains thinking we are actually smelling them!

- Having powerful brains is a great tool for when we are feeling angry or upset. If we are in a situation where we start to feel out of control, we can imagine being in a completely different situation, with different sights, smells, sounds, tastes, and textures that can help calm us.

- We are going to complete an activity today that can help us experience this. I would like for you to look through these magazines, and then tear out one picture that makes you feel SO nice and happy when you look at it. Since this is your first time doing this activity, I will tear out a picture too. *(I always model this the first time, but for future sessions I just have the clients choose a picture.)*

- *(I chose a picture of a field of flowers.)* Now that we both have our pictures, we are going to do a powerful brain activity using our imagination. We are going to count to three, and at three, we are going to pretend that we are jumping into the picture!

Since we are jumping into my picture first, I will be the one to tell you what we are seeing/smelling/touching/tasting/hearing. When it is your picture you, will do all of the telling.

- Once I am finished, we will count to three and then jump out of the picture. We can then talk about how we feel.

- Are you ready? 1-2-3, let's jump in the picture!

  o (My sample script: "We are now in a field of beautiful red and yellow tulips. We see the blue sky, the beautiful flowers, the green grass, and the black birds. We see other children running in the flowers, laughing and having fun. We see our family sitting at a park pavilion getting ready to cook. We hear the birds cawing, the children laughing, and the wind rustling the grass. We hear our family talking about what they are going to cook! We suddenly smell hamburgers and know that is what we will be eating for lunch! We also smell chocolate and realize that we will be eating chocolate cake for dessert. We touch the flower petals, and they are a bit dewy, and oh so soft. We feel the wind blow on our bodies and it helps us stay cool. It's now time to eat, and we run to our families and eat the most delicious hamburgers and chips. We finish just in time to eat a large slice of chocolate cake. It has simply been the best day ever, but it's now time to go. 1-2-3!")

- Now it's your turn! When you're ready please count to three.

  o (Client shares our experiences.)

- Now that we are finished, how did you feel before/during/after this activity? Tell me more about what you noticed. Do you believe you are calmer now? Could this picture help remind you of our time spent together? Would you like to place it in your sensory bag and use whenever needed?

Sensory ABCs

This intervention is a fun way to discover sensory items that begin with letters of the alphabet! The goal is for the children to be mindfully thinking about their senses and things that attract their senses. It's completely acceptable for children to name something that doesn't start with their chosen letter!

MATERIALS: ABC cards are needed for this activity (I made my own with ABC stickers and index cards). Treats can be on hand as well. (I have some index cards with sticker hearts on them. If children pick a heart card, then they get a small treat!)

INSTRUCTIONS:

- As we've discussed before, we can REALLY calm down by using our senses. Our brains are very powerful, so just THINKING about certain sights/smells/sounds/touches/tastes can help us feel better!

- Today we are going to play a sensory card game. Each of these index cards has a letter of the alphabet on it. There are also some index cards that have hearts on them. Each of us will take turns picking a card. If we pick a letter card, we try to name a sight/sound/smell/taste/touch that begins with that letter. Now, some letters, like "X" are difficult, so we can always draw again if we need to! If we draw a heart card we get a little treat! We will play this for at least four rounds, and then we can choose to stop or continue. Let's play!

- *(I typically go first to model, and for this example will pretend I drew a "T.")* Okay, I drew the letter "T." Let me think...I could see a **train**, I could hear a **trumpet**, I could smell a **tulip**, I could taste **toast,** and I could feel **tissue paper**. How did I do? Now it's your turn!

- Now that we are finished, was this activity easy or difficult for you? Did you notice how you had to focus on your thinking? Could you actually see/hear/smell/taste/touch any of the items in your mind while thinking about them? Is there a way you could modify this activity for home or school without the ABC cards?

Cube Roll

This is a simple activity I typically play with younger children. They seem to love rolling the large foam cube and get excited thinking about their senses. If I'm short on time due to having to focus on other priorities in the session, or if I have a child come in to the session looking highly dysregulated, this is my go to intervention!

MATERIALS: A large foam cube is needed for this intervention. I purchase a blank cube (easily found online), and then write one of the words "eyes/ears/nose/mouth/hands/free space" on each of the cube's faces. I also draw a simple drawing of each body part. This can be done with a permanent marker.

INSTRUCTIONS:

- Sometimes children come into the playroom feeling really upset. They could have had a stressful day or are feeling sad about something. It's hard to focus on our goals or to even have fun when we are feeling this way!

- When children come in feeling like this, I suggest we play the game Cube Roll.

- Can I teach you how to play? It's a simple and fun way to begin feeling calmer, more mindful, and more aware of the safety we have in this room.

- Here is a foam cube. It's large, isn't it? You'll notice I have written a body part on each face and have also drawn a picture. The object of this game is to take turns rolling the cube. Since it's a foam cube, we can toss it pretty hard, as long as we don't throw it at each other!

- Next, we check to see what word/picture is facing up, then stop, take three seconds to experience that sense right here, right now, then call out what we experienced. If the cube lands on "free space," then we can give each other a handshake, a hug, or a high five!

- I'll start to show you how to play. I'm going to roll the cube now! It landed on "nose" and what a silly picture of a bunny nose! *(I'm better at drawing animal parts than human parts!)* I will now stop, close my eyes, and take three seconds to smell… I noticed that I smell peppermint, probably because I have peppermint oil diffusing right now.

- Now it's your turn to roll the cube. *(We repeat this four to six times.)*

- Now that we are finished with the game, how are you feeling?

- Do you feel a different feeling than when you first came in here or the same?

- Were any of the senses harder to experience than others?

- Did pausing for three seconds help you sense things better?

- Are there other times where pausing can help us sense what's around us and help us calm?

- When and where?

Sensory Song

I discovered this song several years ago online, with no reference attached. I have tried to find the creator so I can properly credit it to him/her but have not been successful in finding who it is. It is a wonderful song, and young children love to sing along with me when I sing it to them.

MATERIALS: Sensory Song script is all that is needed for this activity.

INSTRUCTIONS:

- Sometimes when we feel nervous, it can help to pay attention to what is right in front of us. If we can focus on what we see, hear, smell, touch, and taste right here, right now, it helps us focus and calm our bodies.

- We can also think about pleasant sights, sounds, smells, touches, and tastes that we love, and that really helps us feel better, too! Our brains are so powerful that if I think really hard about smelling chocolate chip cookies, I will actually be smelling them even though they aren't here!

- I have a song I would love to sing to you! There are parts where I need your help. Please add in something you see, hear, smell, touch, taste, and feel. If you have trouble with any of the senses that are in this room, feel free to choose anything! *(I then sing the song to them.)*

- Great job! How do you feel now?

- Do you think you could sing this song at other places?

- Maybe teach it to others so they can help calm too?

Sensory Song

(Sung to the tune of "The Farmer in the Dell")

I use my eyes to see
I use my eyes to see
And when I want to see a _____
I use my eyes to see

I use my ears to hear
I use my ears to hear
And when I want to hear a _____
I use my ears to hear

I use my nose to smell
I use my nose to smell
And when I want to smell a _____
I use my nose to smell

I use my hands to touch
I use my hands to touch
And when I want to touch a _____
I use my hands to touch

I use my mouth to taste
I use my mouth to taste
And when I want to taste a _____
I use my mouth to taste

Lava Bead Bracelets

Smell can be very relaxing to children, and I often use this sense when looking for a way for clients to regulate in a variety of settings. Creating a lava bead bracelet is an easy way for clients to use their sense of smell in an unobtrusive way when they are feeling dysregulated.

MATERIALS: Lava beads, regular beads, a selection of essential oils (peppermint, lemon, orange, lavender, Ylang Ylang, and vanilla are popular with most children), a stretchy cord, a cotton ball, and scissors are needed for this activity.

INSTRUCTIONS:

- It's important to have strategies for how to calm when we are feeling stressed. We don't want to let our stress get too high or then we can feel out of control.

- All of us need tools to help us feel calmer throughout the day— even grown-ups! It's perfectly normal to have items with us that help us calm down.

- Smelling relaxing scents can be very helpful with calming ourselves. Smells are very individual—what I like to smell may be very different than what you like to smell!

- Today we are going to make a lava bead bracelet. Lava beads are wonderful because they soak in oils for days!

- Here you'll notice I have a cord, lava beads, and regular beads on the craft table. You can cut the stretchy cord then put on as many beads as you'd like. I recommend no more than three of the lava beads so the smell isn't too much for you. When you are finished, we will then test out the oils.

- Now that you are finished, let's test the oils. Remember that we don't need to put our nose directly on the bottle since the scents can be quite strong when in the bottle! *(I only use therapeutic-grade oils that have been tested and are safe for children.)* You can choose which oils you would like to smell from this selection, and then you can smell your choices. I would use the same oil on each lava bead since some oils don't smell very good together.

- Now that you have chosen your scent, let's take this cotton ball and place a few drops of oil on it. We can now cover the lava beads with the oil. Look at how the oil goes right into the bead and doesn't make the bead feel oily!

- You can now take your bracelet home and wear it whenever you feel you may need some help regulating. If your parents have oils, you can reapply oil to the beads every other day or so. If they do not have oils, you can bring your bracelet back anytime and we can reapply here.

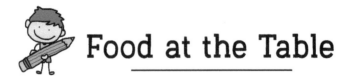 # Food at the Table

The act of sharing food can be a beautiful way of connecting with our clients. In many cultures, gathering together to share a meal is a spiritual and bonding experience. A small snack, experienced with all of our senses and eaten mindfully, can be very calming as well. I share snacks often with my clients (first being mindful to look at my client forms to see if there are any food sensitivities), always using this intervention when we do.

MATERIALS: A small fruit that can easily be cut or sectioned and small ramekins are needed for this activity. I typically use Cuties oranges since they can be peeled and sectioned easily, but I have also used grapes and bananas (a plastic knife is needed for bananas).

INSTRUCTIONS:

- Sometimes the best way to calm our minds and bodies is to have a small snack. We may think that a snack should be candy or chips, but eating healthy fruit and vegetables is so good for our bodies and our minds! Also, if we eat our food very mindfully and with all of our senses, we will notice how wonderful these foods taste!

- We are going to take this orange and experience it with all of our senses. Sounds weird, huh? Well, it can be done!

- Let me peel this orange and give each of us one segment in our ramekin. We will just focus on one segment of the orange for this experience, but we can eat the rest of the orange when finished.

- We are now going to experience this orange with our eye sense. What color is this orange? Is it really all orange? What other colors do we see? Do we notice any lines, dots, or ridges? Any patterns or shapes? Tell me all that you see.

- Now let's experience this orange with our nose sense. Take a nice, long sniff of this orange segment. What do you smell? Is it fruity, sweet, or fresh? Does it smell juicy or tangy? What words could you use to describe the smell of this orange?

- Let's move on to our ear sense. Can this orange make noise? Maybe if we help it out, it can! What does the segment sound like when we tap on it? Drop it into the ramekin? Roll it around in the ramekin? Is it soft or loud? How would you describe its sound?

- Now on to the hand sense. Let's gently touch our orange segment. How does it feel? Soft or hard? Smooth or bumpy? Wet or dry? Describe how it feels.

- Finally, the mouth sense! This is the one we are most used to! But, we will experience this a little differently this time. Please take one bite of the orange segment, then chew for at least 10 chews before swallowing. Now that we've swallowed, how did it taste? Sweet or sour? Dry or juicy? Did the taste change with each chew? How so or not so?

- We may now finish this segment, then eat the rest of the segments. No need to complete this experience with every segment for we should already be feeling very calm in our bodies!

- Try this at home with lots of the foods you eat. You really only need to do it once, and then enjoy the rest of the food at your own pace. You may notice that healthier food actually tastes better to you when trying this!

Cotton Ball Scent

This intervention is similar to the Lava Bead Bracelets but for clients who do not want to wear jewelry. This intervention typically goes into the Sensory Bag when complete.

MATERIALS: A cotton ball, variety of essential oils (as described with The Lava Bead Intervention), and a snack size plastic bag are needed for this intervention.

INSTRUCTIONS:

Directions are explained as if we are completing the Sensory Bag intervention and are at the part where we focus on our noses.

- Now, let's think about our noses. Did you know that our noses need breaks, too? Well, they do! We may smell several things throughout our day, some scents that smell great to us, some that smell horrible!

- Our noses can really help us calm down when we are starting to feel stressed. If we stop and smell something good to us, taking that "nose break" can really help us feel better!

- Notice I have several essential oils sitting on the table. Which do you think you may like? Maybe you wish to smell all of them or maybe just a couple. The choice is up to you! Remember that essential oils in the bottle are stronger than when you put a few drops on something, so there is no need to put your nose right on the bottle. A little sniff will do. Please let me know which oils you would like to smell, and I will screw off the cap and hold the bottle for you. *(I've learned this the hard way after having expensive bottles of oils dropped and spilled!)*

- I see you have picked the oil that you like! We will now take five or six drops of this oil and put it on the cotton ball. Once we are done with this, we will then put the cotton ball in the snack bag and zip it up!

- If you can keep the bag closed for a few hours, the next time you open it, it will smell so nice! This scent will last for over a week!

- We can put this small bag into your sensory bag and then continue with the rest of the senses. Remember, if you ever need a "nose break," you can simply open this snack bag and smell this wonderful scent!

17

Improvisational Interventions

Improvisation (Improv) is one of the most perfect ways of teaching children how to be in the moment, have fun, and learn valuable social skills. A recent NPR broadcast highlighted researchers discovering that using improv with children on the autism spectrum was increasing their ability to recognize, show, and read emotion—skills that are often difficult for these children to do. Since listening to that broadcast, I have been using improv with my clients and experiencing great success!

I have included two scripts in this chapter that I initially use to introduce the concept of improv to my clients. Before I created these scripts, my clients seemed hesitant about the total non-directive approach to improv and wanted to know what to do. Since creating these, my clients are able to take the small bit of direction and go with it in ways I would have never imagined. Be prepared for a lot of laughter and genuine silliness with this activity!

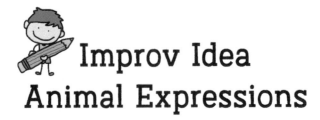

Improv Idea
Animal Expressions

In this improvisation, the client will choose one of the following:

1. Animal

2. Place

3. Object

4. Feeling

The therapist and child will now begin an improv routine in which only the animal, place, object, and feeling are decided ahead of time. This can turn out very differently each time it is done! I allow a great deal of flexibility with improv routines, but "my character" often suggests healthy and safe actions if I feel the client may be getting stuck.

The "Improv Animal Expressions" sheet is a great tool to keep nearby if the client needs any reminders of the structure of the improv. Therapists need to be prepared to get VERY silly!

Improv Animal Expressions

The animal is a/an :

The place is :

The object is :

The feeling is :

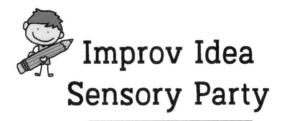

Improv Idea
Sensory Party

In this improvisation, the client will choose each of the following:

1. Two senses

2. One place

3. One object

4. Two feelings

With this improv routine, clients choose two senses, and each of us will play the role of the body part that experiences that sense. The client then chooses the place, the object, and two feelings that can be experienced. We do not set up any other ground rules, and just go with where the improvisational activity takes us! I've noticed that each body part sometimes only experiences one feeling, and other times the clients decide that the body part feels both depending on what it is experiencing. I am careful in improv to have the clients lead the flow of the activity, by only adding to their ideas. There are times "my character" may ask questions to get more information. As with the other improvisation activity in this book, you will never have two of the same experiences. This is such a fun way to work with clients!

The "Improv Sensory Party!" sheet is a great tool to keep nearby if the client needs any reminders of the structure of the improv. Therapists need to be prepared to get VERY silly!

Improv Sensory Party!

The two senses are :

and

The object is :

The two feelings are :

and

Improv Idea
Animal Sounds

This is a much less structured improv activity. Oftentimes, it does not become a story, but more of a turn-taking activity. It is so fun to hear the noises that are created from this intervention!

MATERIALS: A variety of puppets are needed for this intervention.

INSTRUCTIONS:

- All right, it's improv time! I would like for you to choose three puppets. The only rule to choosing is that I want you to choose puppets that you don't know what kind of sound they make. For example, we all know a dog says "Ruff, ruff!" But, do we know what sound a giraffe makes? Or that a pink and purple monster puppet makes? So, we will each choose three puppets that don't have a sound that we know of.

- Great job! We each chose three puppets, so we have six puppets who don't have a sound. How are we going to do an improv activity if they don't make noise? We could have them talk, but that could be kind of boring.

- I've got it! Let's use our imagination and make up sounds for each of these puppets! Since none of them have an actual sound, we can make up whatever sound we want! It can be loud or soft, high or low pitched, short or long! There is no wrong way to do this, and the sillier the better!

- *(The client and I take turns creating sounds for each puppet.)* Oh boy, was that fun! I don't remember the last time I laughed so hard! This was definitely improv since we were really using our imaginations!

- We can now make up a routine based on their sounds or be done with the activity since we were already so creative. This is your choice.

Final Thoughts

To be successful, the first thing to do is fall in love with your work.
—Sister Mary Lauretta

Writing a book is a laborious process. Writing a book based upon your life's passion of play therapy is a labor of love. I am fully aware of the great gift I have been given of being able to work with the most vulnerable of children. I consider it an honor to be a partner in my clients' journeys towards success and healing. I also consider it a gift to be able to meet my therapeutic colleagues through the play therapy trainings I conduct. I am confident that some of the most loving and passionate people are my play therapy brothers and sisters! We are indeed making the world a better place with each child we help nurture and grow.

I sincerely hope that this book gives you some help and support for creating mindful sessions with your clients. I hope the interventions that I have detailed are beneficial for both you and the children you counsel. I invite you to try them first yourself before ever introducing them to your clients. We cannot expect mindful clients if we ourselves are not mindful; what better way to practice than through the use of play!

Please feel free to modify these interventions in whatever ways work for you, and share your ideas with others! We should never be stingy with our knowledge and should openly share with anyone who seeks to become more competent in the field. Because we are all both beginners and experts, and can learn so much from not only each other, but from the beautiful children we encounter.

It is my hope that you have found this book to be both practical and insightful on how to better meet the emotional needs of your clients. I am thankful that I was able to write it, and to share it with you. Best wishes on your journey towards creating more mindful and healthy children!

References

Association for Play Therapy. (2016). *Why Play Therapy?* Retrieved from http://www.a4pt.org.

Baer, R., Smith, G., Hopkins, J., Krietemeyer, J., & Toney, L. (2006). Using self-report assessment methods to explore facets of mindfulness. *Assessment, 13*(1), 27.

Balonon-Rosen, P. (2017). *Using Improv to Help Kids with Autism Show and Read Emotion.* Retrieved from http://www.npr.com.

Beauchemin, J., Hutchins, T., & Patterson, F. (2008). Mindfulness meditation may lessen anxiety, promote social skills, and improve academic performance among adolescents with learning disabilities. *Complementary Health Practice, Volume 13, Issue 1*, pages 34-45.

Beer, M., Ward, L., & Moar, K. (2013). The relationship between mindful parenting and distress in parents of children with an autism spectrum disorder. *Mindfulness, 4*(2), 102-112.

Berzin, R. (2012). *A Simple Breathing Exercise to Calm Your Mind and Body.* Retrieved from http://www.mindbodygreen.com.

Centers for Disease Control and Prevention. (2017). *Autism Spectrum Disorder (ASD).* Retrieved from http://cdc.gov.

Davidson R. J., Kabat-Zinn, J., & Schumacher, J., et al. (2003). Alterations in brain and immune function produced by mindfulness meditation. *Psychosomatic Medicine, 65*, 564-570.

Greenberg, M. T., & Harris, A. R. (2012). Nurturing mindfulness in children and youth: Current state of research. *Child Development Perspectives, 6*, 161-166.

Kabat-Zinn, J. (1997). *Wherever You Go, There You Are: Mindfulness Meditation in Everyday Life.* New York, NY: Hyperion.

Kabat-Zinn, J. (1992). *Full Catastrophe Living: Using the Wisdom of Your Body and Mind to Face Stress, Pain, and Illness.* New York, NY: Random House.

Landreth, G. (2012). *Play Therapy: The Art of the Relationship* (3rd ed.). New York, NY: Taylor and Francis Publishing.

Langer, E., & Djikic, M. (2012). Mindfulness as a psychological attractor: The effect on children. *Journal of Applied Social Psychology, 42*, 114-122.

Ma, S. H., & Teasdale, J. D. (2004). Mindfulness-based cognitive therapy for depression: Replication and exploration of differential relapse prevention effects. *Journal of Consulting and Clinical Psychology, 72*, 31-40.

Nadeau, K. (2017). *The ADHD Test for Girls*. Retrieved from http://www.additude.com.

Nhat Hanh, T. (1996). *The Miracle of Mindfulness: An Introduction to the Practice of Meditation*. Boston, MA: Beacon Press.

Razza, R., Bergen-Cico, D., & Raymond, K. (2013). Enhancing preschoolers' self-regulation via mindful yoga. *Journal of Child and Family Studies, 24*, 372-385.

Sawyer Cohen, J., & Semple, R. (2009). Mindful parenting: A call for research. *Journal of Child and Family Studies, 19*, 145-151.

Turner-Bumberry, T. (2015). *Finding Meaning with Mandalas: A Therapist's Guide to Creating Mandalas with Children*. Saint Charles, MO: Turner Phrase Publishing LLC.